Books by Richard B. Wright

A Life with Words

A Writer's Memoir

RICHARD B. WRIGHT

PHYLLIS BRUCE EDITIONS

SIMON & SCHUSTER CANADA

New York London Toronto Sydney New Delhi

Simon & Schuster Canada
A Division of Simon & Schuster, Inc.
166 King Street East, Suite 300
Toronto, Ontario M5A 1J3

Special thanks to the Giller Prize Foundation for the use of the
essay "Finding Clara," published by Penguin Canada in the 2003
Scotiabank Giller Prize Anthology of Canadian Fiction.

The excerpt from *The Weekend Man* is taken from the 2001
edition published by HarperCollins Canada.

The excerpt from *Adultery* is taken from the 2004 edition
published by HarperCollins Canada.

This Simon & Schuster Canada edition September 2015

SIMON & SCHUSTER CANADA and colophon are
registered trademarks of Simon & Schuster, Inc.

For information about special discounts for bulk purchases,
please contact Simon & Schuster Special Sales at
1-800-268-3216 or CustomerService@simonandschuster.ca.

Manufactured in the United States of America

1 3 5 7 9 10 8 6 4 2

Library and Archives Canada Cataloguing in Publication

Wright, Richard B., 1937–, author
A life with words / Richard B. Wright.
Issued in print and electronic formats.
1. Wright, Richard B., 1937–. 2. Authors, Canadian (English)—
20th century—Biography. I. Title.
PS8595.R6Z47   2015
C818'.5409   C2015-903846-4
C2015-903847-2

ISBN 978-1-4767-8534-9
ISBN 978-1-4767-8536-3 (ebook)

*To my wife, Phyllis, who shared
the journey and was of inestimable help
along the way*

Contents

Author's Note

Memory is only one version of the truth about a life and I have tried to get as close to the truth as an aging writer's memory allows. Some names have been changed.

A Life with Words

The Boy in the Well

Hey, diddle, diddle,
The cat and the fiddle,
The cow jumped over the moon;
The little dog laughed
To see such sport,
And the dish ran away with the spoon.

Sitting beside him on the bed, his mother recited the words while he lay waiting for the sandman to sprinkle the magic powder over his eyes. Meanwhile, he listened again to the words. How old was he? Old enough to understand that words could put pictures in your head. Perhaps he was five. In his mind's eye he saw the cat on his hind legs wearing blue trousers with a grey vest and brown coat. Had he dressed the cat in his imagination, or was he remembering a picture on the wall of a store downtown where they sold toys and clothes for children? That was even earlier and he was very little then; his father was carrying him and there was snow falling on the street. Beyond the store's big front window people were hurrying past with snow on their hats. It was the time of the year when Santa Claus came with presents. But perhaps looking at his mother and listening to the words, he thought he had invented his own version of the cat

3

looking pleased with himself as he amused the dog, while high above them in a vast, dark sky a tiny cow was leaping across the moon, and the Man in the Moon was offering a wide grin to the earth below, where hand in hand, the dish and the spoon were running off to a forest. It was all a bit silly, he supposed, but it was funny too and made him smile and he liked the sound of the words in his ears. Sometimes, though, his mother read words from a book and the pictures they made in his head disturbed him.

Rock-a-bye, baby,
Thy cradle is green,
Father's a nobleman,
Mother's a queen
And Betty's a lady
And wears a gold ring
And Johnny's a drummer
And drums for the king.

Hush-a-bye, baby,
On the treetop,
When the wind blows,
The cradle will rock,
When the bough breaks,
The cradle will fall,
Down will come baby,
Bough, cradle and all.

He liked the first part describing the happy family and Johnny who drummed for the king. He thought that one day he too might like to play a drum for the king. But the second part frightened him, and each time he listened, he wondered why they put the baby in the cradle at the top of a tree with the wind blowing. Yet he never thought to ask his mother until many years later when he had become a writer of fiction, and on a visit to his mother's home had referred to the poem and joked that perhaps this was the beginning of his lifelong struggle with anxiety. "What would you have said, Ma, if I had asked you why they put that baby in a cradle way up in the treetop when the forecast called for wind?"

She had frowned, looking perhaps for a hint of criticism about her child rearing. He surmised that she was carefully arranging her answer. Finally, she replied, "I would have said that people can be careless."

"Ah, a cautionary tale then?"

"If that's what you call it. I don't understand why you are bringing up nursery rhymes. They are only old stories, for Heaven's sake."

And she *was* right. They were only old stories, and if he was inclined all those years ago to enter fully into them, it wasn't her fault. At that early age he had come to accept that not all stories end happily. Humpty Dumpty had fallen off his wall too, and broken into so many pieces that he could not be put together again. Life couldn't get much worse than that. Sometimes children also fell; they fell into rivers and lakes and gullies. He once heard his mother and father talking about a boy who had leaned too far over, and fallen into an old, dry well on someone's farm. The unfortunate child lay in the dark for days before they found him, and, of course, he was dead. His mother seemed drawn to such terrible stories; her pessimistic cast of mind, almost willingly it seemed to him, accepted catastrophe as a part of life. Each night after storytelling time, she took his left hand in hers and together they recited the prayer,

> *Now I lay me down to sleep,*
> *I pray the Lord my soul to keep.*
> *If I should die before I wake,*
> *I pray the Lord my soul to take.*

To him too the world seemed dangerous. He knew, for instance, that somewhere—in a place called overseas—a war was going on, and he listened intently on the fringes of conversations his parents had with friends and neighbours about fathers and sons and nephews of people in town who were fighting the Germans overseas. He also heard voices on the big radio in the living room talking about the war. Some people his parents mentioned would not be coming home ever because they had been killed. Death, he learned, was out there waiting for everyone. Once he asked his mother what happened when you died. What happened to the boy in the well or the soldiers overseas who were shot dead in the fighting? His mother told him that when good people died, they went to Heaven, which was way up in the sky, and one evening, after a day of rain when the sky was clearing, she took him outside to see a colourful sunset. The sky was full of radiant light. God, she told him, was painting the sky, and as he looked up at the light streaming through the clouds, she said, "And that's where Heaven is, way up behind those clouds." But he was not consoled. He did not want to live behind the clouds in the sky and he did not like the idea of his mother and father or his sister and brothers dying and going up there either. A small, watchful boy, he especially worried about his father, who had been a soldier in another war long ago, but was now part of something called the Home Guard.

Two evenings a week his father put on his soldier's uniform of rough brown cloth and left for the curling rink. The cloth scratched the boy's cheeks when his father picked him up to say goodbye, always adding the little rhyme *Now sleep tight/Don't let the bedbugs bite.* He liked the little rhyme, and he knew it was just a joke. There were no bugs in his bed. His mother wouldn't stand for that. He liked to watch his father use a cloth to polish his big boots and then wrap the puttees—which he thought a strange word—around his legs and then put on his soldier's cap adjusted to a jaunty angle. Now he was ready to walk to the curling rink a few blocks away and drill for two hours with veterans of that earlier war. When he was older the boy would be told that the Home Guard was there to protect the shipyard and the four grain elevators from German sabotage. He liked the sound of that word too and at night lay in bed imagining one of the elevators or the shipyard exploding, the flames lighting the sky. But on those evenings when his father put on his soldier's uniform, he worried about him and one evening convinced himself that, if his father left the house, he would not return but go overseas to fight the Germans and be killed and go up beyond the clouds to live. And so, as his father was putting the final touches on his boots, the boy hurried along the hallway and stood there with his back against the front door, his arms splayed out behind him, barring the way to a dangerous world, a small, furious figure bent on throwing a tantrum if his father left the house. After his father whispered the bedbug rhyme in his ear and handed him over to one of his brothers—he can no longer remember which one—he began to wail. He had got himself into what his mother would have called "a state." Where was his mother? Visiting a neighbour perhaps. But what a fuss he made there by the front door! His brother was right to be disgusted with him.

After their father left he continued to cry and said that his daddy was going to the overseas place and the Germans would kill him. His brother gave him a little push. "Oh, stop bawling and don't be such a dope. Dad's only going to the curling rink."

When his mother came home they couldn't find him. They called his name and he could hear his mother scolding his brother for not looking after him. They found him finally in the basement crouching behind the furnace.

Toward the end of her long life, in the winter of 1993, his mother gave him a yellowing envelope that still bore a stale fragrance from the cedar chest where she had stored her keepsakes. In the envelope were a few small black and white snapshots; they were probably taken by his mother's younger sister, his aunt Clara, for he has no memory of there being a camera in their house. Aunt Clara and Uncle Harry visited once or twice a year. Uncle Harry had a good job with the Hydro and they owned a car, a 1939 Dodge, a source of wonder to him when he sat behind the big steering wheel and pretended he was driving. Looking at those black and white photographs years later always left him with a brief and almost unbearable sadness.

One of the photographs was taken early in the war years, probably not long before he tried to save his father's life in the front hall. In the photo, the boy is standing by a small rock garden at the front of their rented house on Queen Street in Midland, Ontario, a grave-looking little fellow in a suit with short pants, a handkerchief tucked nattily into the suit's upper coat pocket. He is not exactly frowning, but neither is he looking particularly pleased about having his picture taken. It is easy to imagine him refusing to smile by shaking his head enough times to discourage the photographer. Just as his mother always did when asked to "Please try to look a little happier, Laura." The attitude toward picture taking by both mother and son could perhaps be best summed up as "Take me as I am or forget about it."

The author in 1941 at age four.

Looking at the little black and white photograph so many years later, he concentrated on the boy's hands; the right one seems to be tucked into a pocket of his suit coat while the other hangs by his left side. A picture taken then before the onset of the self-consciousness that would consume him in the first decades of his life, when appearance and self-regard are so important. Never again would his left hand be exposed to a camera. In those days it was called a webbed hand, the little finger a mere stump of flesh, the three middle fingers joined together and radically shortened by some genetic train wreck at conception. Mercifully, the thumb was normal, allowing him at least to grasp things, making the hand, if decidedly odd-looking, at least partially useful. Later in life his mother would tell him quite without embarrassment that after his birth she spent a week in St. Andrew's Hospital and all that time she concealed his "little hand" while receiving visitors. On another floor of the hospital his father was painting rooms to pay the bill. Or so the family legend has it, and it may well have been true, for it was 1937 and the Great Depression was far from over: his father had been laid off work at a dress factory and was making do by raking leaves in the town's park and painting hospital rooms. The appearance of a fifth child didn't appear to bother him in the least. Nor did the fact that his youngest son had a deformed hand, though he entertained peculiar notions of how it might have come about. When he was ten or eleven, the boy overheard his father in another room telling a visitor that the deformity may well have been caused by a bat. Yes, a bat, which had entered their bedroom one night early in his wife's pregnancy. Of course it frightened her, and, as anyone could see, the boy's hand was bat-like in shape. For a while, he himself believed this preposterous explanation.

When he was six and entered school, however, he began to see how people with far more serious handicaps were getting on with their lives as best they could: the boy in grade three stricken with polio and confined to a wheelchair; the red-faced, stammering child attempting to read aloud a passage of poetry amid the snickers of classmates and the hateful frown of his teacher, who had insisted that he get on with it; the girl who dragged the heavy shoe on her club foot through the hallways, trying to ignore the imitations of her awkward gait by those following her; the large, ungainly boy whose encephalitis had damaged his brain and trapped him in an early grade with younger children half his size. In the classrooms and schoolyards of the 1940s, he would see plenty of evidence that life could hand out some very raw deals. Still he was angered by the eyes gawking at his hand and so he got used to concealing it.

The war brought death to soldiers and sailors and the men who flew airplanes, but it also brought work to those at home. After years of odd jobs, his father found steady employment in one of the grain elevators where ships filled with wheat and oats and barley from the Prairie Provinces came down through the Great Lakes from Fort William and Port Arthur to Midland, where the grain was unloaded and shipped by rail to Toronto and Montreal. All this his father would later explain to him. He liked hearing about the grain travelling by boats and boxcars to feed people. The elevator was often busy and his father sometimes worked two shifts in a row, leaving in the morning with three lunches and working through the night and into another day. All this extra work meant more money, and the boy now knew that money was important. Nor did his father ever complain about the extra shifts he had to work. He was just glad to have a job that paid more than raking leaves in the town park.

At night, reciting the words of that terrible prayer about dying before waking, the boy could hear faintly the riveting guns at the shipyard, where they were building boats for the war. His father told him that these boats were called corvettes and would be used to sink German submarines in the North Atlantic.

By now he could read a little and write his name, and sometimes he sat at the kitchen table like his brothers pretending that he was working on homework. Then one year at the end of the summer, he walked with his mother to Regent School, and after she left, he stood with all the other children milling about the schoolyard and softball diamond, chattering, waiting for the teachers to come out and sort them into lineups by grade, listening to the shrieks of the girls from the other side of the school. Soon he was being pushed ahead in the grade one boys line, entering the place where he would see the boy with the large head and the vacant eyes and the club-footed girl.

The house they lived in on Queen Street was their third rental, and one evening in late February of 1944, when he was nearly seven, the owner, Mr. Perkins, came to the back door. When the boy answered it, a small balding man in a brown leather windbreaker asked to see his parents, who were in the living room listening to *Amos 'n' Andy* on the radio. He could hear laughter from time to time. *Amos 'n' Andy* was his father's favourite program. When his mother came into the kitchen, he could see her surprise at seeing Mr. Perkins standing in a puddle of mud. She frowned at the mud on her kitchen floor, and he reluctantly removed his galoshes and followed her into the living room. She usually saw him only on the first day of the month, when the rent was due. His mother was proud of her cleanliness. Cleanliness was next to godliness. One of the many truisms she often took out, dusted off and presented as evidence of a particular position. After his mother closed the door, he could no longer hear the radio or the laughter and so he sat at the kitchen table reading a storybook. Where were his brothers that night? They seemed to be out a great deal in the evenings and they no longer worked much on homework at the kitchen table. His brother Jim, who was nine years older, would soon get a job on one of the freighters as a deckhand. His sister, Joyce, who was twelve years older, would go to Toronto to work at Eaton's, leaving Bill, seven years older, and Douglas, four years older.

So alone he listened to the murmuring voices as he tried to read his book. He didn't like Mr. Perkins, who should have taken off his galoshes before he came into the kitchen. It wasn't long before Perkins opened the door and walked past him without a word, zipping up his windbreaker and stooping to put on his galoshes, buckling them and leaving. His father and mother then came into the kitchen. His father looked tired and unhappy and went upstairs without a word while his mother sat down at the kitchen table across from him. There were tears in her eyes and this troubled him. She told him then that they would have to move because Mr. Perkins was going into the poultry business and, since he worked as a cook on one of the lake freighters, he wanted to get his business under way before the start of the shipping season; therefore he would be using their basement as a hatchery within the week. When he asked what a hatchery was, she told him as best she could about the rearing of chickens.

They had to be out of the house by the first of April, only six weeks away, and finding a house would not be easy. In later years he would come to think of his mother as the Queen of All Pessimistic Souls. But perhaps at the time she had reason to be downhearted. The war had brought money into the town, but it had also brought people from outlying villages and farms to work at the shipyard and the foundry; the woollen mill and the grain elevators. Whole families were moving into town and rental properties were scarce. Buying a house, she told him, was out of the question even if one were available, because they couldn't afford it. From there, of course, she made her habitual leap into extravagant despair. "It wouldn't surprise me at all to see us out on the street with our furniture by the first of April." His poor mother could not see the future in any other way. Nor did she mince words, spare feelings or offer comfort. She had to share the bad news with someone, even her seven-year-old son. This she called "being realistic" when it wasn't anything of the kind; it was just another opportunity to complain about the unfairness of life in general and the burdens it imposed upon her in particular. Why within a few days with those chickens in the basement, there would be a terrible smell from the dust and feathers; they would probably develop respiratory problems.

In many ways he was already used to her exaggerated prophecies of disaster: the pimple that would become a boil, the sore throat that surely foretold the onset of whooping cough or diphtheria. Yet this time it struck him how vulnerable and helpless his mother seemed. The little baldheaded man had entered their house and within ten minutes had disrupted their lives. Later he would nod in agreement as she listed Mr. Perkins's various shortcomings. "Miserable man. I never liked him. From the day I met him I didn't like him, and I told your father as much. Little weasel. And now, after filling the house with dust and chicken feathers, he's putting us out on the street." Now he could also picture them cowering amid the furniture on a street corner. Might as well have it raining too.

He was discovering that he was closer to his mother in temperament than he had thought, and so he absorbed her hatred for the landlord, as she called him. A week later when he came home from school, a panel truck was in the driveway and Perkins was carrying trays of eggs down the cellar steps. His mother could not bear to be around the man and was in the living room listening to the radio serial *Pepper Young's Family*. Meanwhile the boy sat at the kitchen table with his reader open watching Perkins stepping carefully down the cellar steps, the trays of eggs and cardboard boxes of chicks in his arms. How easy it would be, he thought, to approach the man from behind on his next trip and with a firm push send him toppling to the cement floor below! He had seen the word *toppling* recently in a book and liked the sound of it. There would be a brief cry from Perkins as he fell with his trays of eggs, and then his head would hit the cement floor, and he would lie amid the blood and crushed eggs and dead chicks. A good end to a bad man who was putting them on the street. It would all look like a terrible accident; the man had too many trays in his arms. He had missed a step and fallen to his doom. "Fallen to his doom." He also liked the sound of those four words. If by chance Perkins survived and claimed that he was pushed, probably by the boy, he would deny it with tears. He would throw a tantrum. Hurl himself onto the kitchen floor with the policemen above him. "I never did. I never did," he would cry.

As the boy watched Perkins go out the door for another armful of trays, he felt such a shiver of fear and excitement that he had to get up and leave the kitchen. Another minute of watching Perkins and he would have been a murderer. Instead he went to the living room and sat on the rug next to his mother and listened to *Pepper Young's Family*. Perhaps another day he would kill Perkins. Years later on a visit home, he asked his mother what became of the landlord and his egg business. "Oh, that," she said with a scornful laugh that always saluted another example of human folly. "It was a complete bust. All his mail-order chickens died. It was just a get-rich-quick scheme. There was a lot of that kind of thing going on during the war." He never told her about his plan to kill Perkins.

Now, with the end of March approaching and no house available, his mother appealed to the occult, enlisting the help of a local seer, Madam Cordova, who lived in a cottage on the edge of town next to a White Rose gas station. Many times his mother would relate how she was met in the candlelit parlour by the prophetess, impressively clad in a purple velvet gown with a gold-coloured turban on her head. For seventy-five cents Madam Cordova would peer into a small opaque globe and foresee what nowadays might be called happy outcomes. She then offered a cup of tea, after which she read the leaves in his mother's cup, expertly diagnosing the source of her visitor's anxiety. "You are looking for shelter, are you not, Mrs. Wright?" This seemed like remarkable prescience, though in hindsight less so since many others were likewise engaged in this quest. Before his mother left, Madam Cordova assured her that she would be successful. To cover her bets, however, his mother also sought Divine help, choosing the Roman Catholic Church as her conduit to God's ear. This was surprising since she often criticized Catholics for moral lapses such as bingo games in the church hall on Sunday afternoons. Still she travelled the three miles in a friend's car to the Martyrs' Shrine to pray and light a candle or two. The famous shrine was dedicated to the memory of the Jesuit missionaries Brébeuf and Lalemant, who were slain there by the Iroquois in 1649.

In the end she was convinced that her success had more to do with Madam Cordova than with the Catholic Church, but it didn't matter; they had finally found a house. Or rather his father had; he'd heard of a large frame home on a corner lot on the west side of town. The house was not for rent, but for sale, and somehow his father, thanks to overtime at the elevator, had managed to save two hundred dollars, which was exactly ten percent of the asking price. According to his mother, "Vern must have charmed the owner, an old lady with a reputation for being *difficult*." This was a backhanded compliment. His mother was happy enough to have a house at last, but she was clearly suspicious of charm in whatever guise.

The only catch to all this was that the house was not available until the first of June. Where could they live in the meantime? By then his sister, Joyce, had gone to Toronto to live with an aunt and work, and his oldest brother, Jim, was on a lake freighter. So that left five of them, his parents, his brothers Bill and Doug, and his small seven-year-old self. The only solution was to rent two cabins at the Tourist Court owned by the proprietor of the White Rose gas station; indeed it may have been Madam Cordova who suggested it. It was early April and there was still snow on the ground. Across the highway was the Catholic cemetery and beyond that the still frozen Little Lake. They used space heaters in the two cabins and his mother cooked on a two-burner hot plate. It was cramped but adequate and everyone was glad to be away from the house on Queen Street with the chickens in the basement: their endless cheeping, the bad air, and perhaps just the singular weirdness of the whole experience.

Yet after a week of cabin life, not surprisingly, his mother decided that she and her youngest child would be better off at her parents' home, in the village of Woodville seventy miles eastward. And so on a Saturday morning his grandfather arrived in his blue 1932 Willys-Overland coupe, a wondrous machine to the child. On the trip he enjoyed watching his grandfather shift the gear lever with his big hand as they moved along Highway 12, the needle on the speedometer registering a steady thirty miles an hour.

He and his mother would spend the next six weeks in the village. He was enrolled in grade two at the local school, where all six grades were in one room, with each grade assigned to a row. After finishing an assignment in his scribbler, he could listen to what older children were learning. His classmates were welcoming and helpful and some became playmates after school. Within a few years, he would make an annual visit to Woodville; in the last weeks of his summer holidays he would travel by train with a small valise and his lunch and a copy of *The Standard*, a Montreal paper, which had the best "funnies," and sometimes also an article about his favourite hockey team, the Montreal Canadiens, who would soon be leaving for training camp. If he was lucky there might be something written about his favourite player, Maurice "Rocket" Richard. After his father stepped down to the platform to wave goodbye, the ten-year-old boy would experience a surge of pure elation; he was by himself now with his sandwiches and his "funnies," and ahead were three hours of reading or looking out the window at the late summer countryside, listening to the conductor call out the names of now long vanished stations: Foxmead, Uptergrove, Brechin, Gamebridge. When he heard the call for Lorneville Junction, it was time to gather together his things because the next stop was Woodville, where his grandfather would be waiting in his Willys coupe to take him to the house and his supper of scrambled eggs and bread and a piece of raspberry pie, with a glass of milk which was sometimes a bit sour, for his grandparents had neither icebox nor refrigerator. He didn't mind that and soon got used to other old-fashioned amenities: the backyard pump, which he loved to use; the privy behind the drive shed, where his grandfather had his workbench and tools.

The house itself and the village would so impress his imagination that more than half a century later it would furnish much of the setting for his most popular novel, *Clara Callan*: the house with its coloured-glass panels in the window of the front door through which he could look out at the street with the trees bathed suddenly in yellow or blue or scarlet light; the wraparound veranda with its hammock where a seven-year-old Clara would watch her younger sister playing with other children while the townspeople looked for their missing mother. In the long afternoons of those summer days, he walked along the railway tracks where in one of the fields Clara would be accosted and raped by the two tramps. Nothing was lost. It was there inside him all those years, emerging finally from his imagination into words.

When he began to publish books, he was sometimes asked if he had ever seen himself at twelve, at sixteen, at twenty, as a novelist one day and he always replied that it never occurred to him then that being a novelist was within his grasp. Perhaps he feared the mockery that might follow such a statement. Growing up in a small Ontario town in the 1940s and '50s, he was conscious of how most people around him regarded outlandish ambition. A young and talented hockey player could say that he would like to make one of the six NHL teams, and while most people might consider that a long shot, they would at least regard it as a reasonable and acceptable goal. But to suggest that one day you would like to sing at the Metropolitan Opera or publish a book would likely be frowned upon; you were being presumptuous, stepping beyond yourself. Or to use one of his mother's favourite expressions, "Just don't get too big for your britches, mister." This provincial disdain for artistic ambition has been well documented in Alice Munro's fiction and summed up perfectly in the title of one of her earlier books, *Who Do You Think You Are?* When he was a child then, the boy's stories were his alone, the characters and what happened to them living only within himself. He had friends and playmates, but often after school, when he was alone, he sought out his own world and told his stories to himself. In the basement of the house on Fifth Street, he walked around playing the parts of various characters, whether they were soldiers in battle or shipwrecked mariners at sea. An odd child, but mercifully left alone by his parents, who sensed that he often wished to retreat into a world of his own making. There were no therapists in those days to consult about his behaviour. His brothers mostly ignored him; he was the mildly goofy kid brother who sometimes talked to himself in the basement. No cause for alarm. On Saturdays, he went to the public library to enter other worlds. The world of horses in *Black Beauty* or pirates in *Treasure Island* or shipwrecks in *Robinson Crusoe*. He rather liked the idea of being marooned. In some way, in his own life, he already was.

His father's workweek ended at noon on Saturday, but sometimes he also worked on Sunday as a watchman, leaving early in the morning to relieve the night man. After Sunday school the boy would take his father's lunch to him along with a sandwich and a piece of pie or cake for himself. He was ten years old and enjoyed those walks along Fifth Street carrying his father's lunch pail, crossing the Penetang road and then past the bush and brook toward the big grey elevator and the boxcars on rail sidings waiting to be filled with grain. His father always watched for him, standing by the door of the little office where he stayed between his rounds. The boy liked the office, with its green blotters on the desks, the pencils and pens and bottles of ink, which he was not allowed to touch. After lunch, while his father read the Saturday *Telegram*, the boy would use one of the long yellow pencils to draw stick figures of characters from

The author on his way
to see his father at the
elevator in 1949.

the Saturday "funnies": the boxer Joe Palooka and his manager, Knobby, the Katzenjammer Kids and Alley Oop. His favourite was *Our Boarding House,* with the magnificently indolent Major Hoople in his smoking jacket and fez trying to avoid his stout, aproned wife and her broom. Above the characters he wrote dialogue in little circles.

When it was time for his father to go on one of the hourly rounds, the boy would go with him, stepping into the little cage where he was allowed to press the button and be jolted as the contraption moved upward, his father pressing the stop button when the cage was exactly level with the next floor. There his father punched a clock, taking a key from a cup chained to a wall and inserting it into the black clock he carried around his neck on a strap. The boy enjoyed going up in the rickety cage but was more apprehensive when they descended, imagining a malfunction in the apparatus that would send them plunging through all that dark space to their deaths. Yet he was fascinated by the big building always quiet on a winter Sunday afternoon, save for a few cooing pigeons roosting on beams overhead. He especially liked reaching the top floor, where he could look down into the huge cement silos filled with wheat or oats or barley, awaiting transport by rail to flour mills. He asked questions about all this and his father answered them and this made the boy proud of his father, who was helping people to have bread to eat. When he said this one day, his father laughed and told him his job was not that important.

From all this, the boy imagined a story about a grain of wheat and its long journey to the silos of that grain elevator. He never took down a word of it, but over many weeks in his imagination, he added details based on what his father had told him. His story was narrated by Wally Wheat, a seed planted on a farm somewhere in the prairies; the boy imagined the Wheat family growing beneath the soil until one early summer day when they emerged into the sunlight, joining millions of others to become a field of wheat. Then the arrival of the harvesting machine to cut them down. It didn't really hurt much, and the threshing machine, which shot them through a big pipe into the back of a truck, was fun for Wally and his brothers and sisters. The truck took them to a rail siding and a boxcar for the trip to a big elevator in Port Arthur or Fort William and by freighter then to where he now stood with his father looking down at them in the silo. Try as he might, he could not devise a happy ending for this tale. He decided that the Wheat family was put on earth to be baked and eaten in a cake or a loaf of bread. The story entertained him for weeks and he was sorry when he finished it.

Oddly enough it surfaced again in his imagination years later when he was in high school, a hapless sixteen-year-old student of biology. When he was asked on an examination to describe and explain the process of wheat germination, his mind drew a blank. The best he could offer was a narrative version of events.

One morning over breakfast, Mrs. Wheat said to her husband, "Walter, I think I'm in the family way."

Along with his well-deserved zero was the teacher's pithy observation, "A typical smart alec answer, Wright. You are an ignoramus in this subject."

Too true, Porky, he thought. And so he would remain for the rest of his life.

*

On a hot summer evening in his twelfth year, he stood outside the Gospel Hall on Second Street reading the announcement board.

Tonight Will Change Your Life
Hear the inspiring words of
Reverend Mel Jackson of Grand Rapids, Michigan

The doors were open, and he watched the people passing through to the lighted hall. Michigan he knew was in America, and at that time in his life he was in love with America. Everything about that country seemed more dramatic and more appealing than Canada. Had Americans not put their broad shoulders to the wheel and helped poor little England and her colonies beat the German bullies? And they beat Tojo and Japan too. He loved American comic books, and on Saturday afternoons at the Capitol Theatre he cheered for American cowboys like Hopalong Cassidy and Roy Rogers. The radio shows he liked best were mostly American: *The Green Hornet, Boston Blackie, The Shadow, Ozzie and Harriet, The Great Gildersleeve.* Hadn't Americans invented Coca-Cola and the automobile? When big passenger ships like the *North American* berthed at the town dock on summer afternoons, weren't the American tourists shopping on King Street better dressed and livelier than the quietly humble townsfolk? When the boat weighed anchor and backed slowly out of the slip, the American passengers in their sundresses and colourful shirts and wide slacks stood along the railing and threw money at the children on the dock who were waving goodbye; dimes and Buffalo nickels were fought over by the scrambling youngsters, and one magical day he picked up a fifty-cent piece. Americans seemed more confident than Canadians. Everyone wanted to live there; they were the envy of the world in 1948.

Grand Rapids, Michigan. He liked the sound of it and followed others into the Gospel Hall and sat on one of the folding metal chairs near the back. The place was nearly full, and in the close, rank air, shirts and dresses stuck to people's backs and women fanned themselves with the programs handed out at the door. In front of him a girl a year or two older in a blouse and dirndl skirt sat with her parents, though she never spoke to them or even looked their way, and he wondered if she had been forced to spend the evening with them. He could see the outline of her brassiere through the blouse. On the stage a middle-aged woman at the piano was playing hymns. He read the words in his program. *Welcome friends and lovers of truth. Heaven awaits you!*

Around him were mostly people who looked poor in their shabby clothes. Some children had impetigo sores that were covered in white ointment. One boy had an eyeful of sties. But an excited murmur ran through the hall as they awaited the words of the American preacher. When the woman stopped playing the piano, a hush fell across the audience as three women and three men walked onto the stage holding their hymnals. They were black and stood smiling out at the audience. The only black people he had ever seen were the cooks and porters wearing white uniforms staring out the portholes of the kitchens on the big passenger ships. He had watched black people in the movies, but they were nearly always comical figures, forever rolling their eyes in fear. They were not real to him. His favourite boxer, Joe

Louis, was real and he was black and the heavyweight champion of the world. When the boy listened to fights on the radio with his father, he always cheered for Joe Louis while his father liked the challenger, a white fighter named Billy Conn. But Joe Louis always won; nobody in the world could beat him.

When the pianist struck a chord, the choir burst into song, and immediately the Reverend Jackson, a burly white man in shirt sleeves, strode across the stage to the lectern clapping his hands above his head. There were sweat stains under his arms, and as he clapped in time to the music, everyone joined in, slowly at first and then rhymically in the spirit of celebration. The words to the hymn were in the program, and soon he was singing with the others. *When the roll is called up yonder, I'll be there.* The clapping and the music filled the hall and he had never heard anything like it. When he attended the Presbyterian church, the singing of hymns was muted, a mere drone above the organ. But there in the Gospel Hall the music was lively and joyful and he felt a sudden and thrilling happiness. When the music stopped and the preacher began to speak, he was soon entranced. Here, he thought, was another use for words: words to appeal and persuade, to capture people's pain and uncertainty, to offer hope and dispel the spectre of death. In front of him the girl was fanning herself. She had not joined in the singing and clapping and at one point had reached into her blouse to adjust the brassiere strap, half glancing backward, dismissing him. But he sensed something powerful in that sullen glance, some apprehension he was not yet ready to understand.

Toward the end of the evening the Reverend Jackson came down from the lectern to implore the people to save themselves by embracing the Lord's promise of eternal life. The pianist began to play and the choir sang, *Softly and tenderly, Jesus is calling/Calling for you and for me,* and the boy stood up and followed others to the front of the hall.

That night an enormous storm broke over the town with rain slashing against windows and drumming on roofs; fierce lightning opened the skies, and he took it as a sign from God that he was now saved. He had always been warned never to stand by a window during a storm, but that night he stood watching the lightning, and letting himself be startled but not frightened by the intense thunder. When his mother came into the bedroom to see if he was all right, she was astonished to see him by the window. He didn't tell her about the Reverend Jackson. Not yet, for that night he wanted to keep all his happiness within. In time all this was forgotten and would not be summoned forth until another century, when he wrote a novel called *Adultery,* in which the protagonist, Dan Fielding, attends a funeral in a small town and recalls an incident in his youth.

It was some kind of Youth for Christ rally in a Sunday school auditorium, and he had followed others into the hall with its old-cupboard smell and its wainscoting and folding metal chairs. There were men in shirt sleeves and women in flowered dresses and boys and girls his age and older teenagers too. The preacher was an American and he talked about godless Communism and the hydrogen bomb, the approaching conflagration, and the love that Jesus had for each and every one of them. He was a stolid-looking man with a dark, receding hairline and a five o'clock shadow. He had taken off his jacket and when he raised his arms to call upon the young to come forth, people could see the sweat marks. A woman in the choir began to sing, "Softly and tenderly, Jesus is calling," and the rest joined in. The American preacher implored them to come forward and embrace their Saviour, and soon people were shifting sideways in their chairs to let others pass. From various parts of the hall, young people stood up and prepared to be saved.

In front of Fielding was a girl about his age in a dirndl skirt and a white blouse. She was with her parents and they looked poor. He had been watching her when she sat farther down the row, but to make room for others she and her parents had moved to seats in front of him. Before they moved, however, Fielding had seen something harsh and unlovely and powerful in the girl's listless gaze. When she was seated in front of him, he could see her bra strap through the blouse and everything was at once unsettling and wonderful: his fight with the rough-looking boy, the long evening light in the auditorium windows, the preacher's words of healing and redemption, the swell of the girl's cheek. When she got up to make her way past the others, she reached behind to pluck the skirt from between her buttocks and a moment later Fielding too arose and followed her up the aisle.

During the first week of the boy's *conversion* the people at the Gospel Hall assigned a mentor to guide him lest he stray from the narrow and difficult path he had chosen, a kind of *buddy system* one now associates with Alcoholics Anonymous. The man lived on First Street with his wife, who served tea and biscuits in the kitchen when he visited them on Sunday afternoons. The mentoring was mostly confined to the handing out of tracts, and the boy sensed the awkwardness in these weekly encounters.

There was very little "buddy" about his mentor, and boy and man both soon discovered that, apart from a shared enthusiasm for their Heaven-bound prospects, they had little to say to one another. And so, as if by mutual consent, they drifted apart, perhaps each recognizing in the other a solitary traveller best left to his own devices.

For his part the eleven-year-old boy was content to read the Gospels without interference from another, and soon he was also drawn to parts of the Old Testament, to the grave and sonorous verses of the Book of Psalms and Proverbs and Ecclesiastes. As he read the Bible, he often imagined himself as a robed figure in dusty sandals with his bag of nuts and figs, his walking staff and wineskin of water, somewhere in the Holy Land en route to Jerusalem to meet the new prophet, the Nazarene called Jesus. Each night after prayers he imagined the next chapter in his character's journey. On Sunday afternoons, remembering the Reverend Jackson, he delivered stirring homilies in his bedroom. It never occurred to him at the time that his behaviour was decidedly odd.

He was, however, not alone in being caught up in this quest for redemption and sanctity. After years of wartime scarcity, people in North America were eager to get on with making their lives more comfortable and, with manufactured goods now available, they were on a buying binge: electric stoves and refrigerators, radio and television sets, vacuum cleaners and automobiles; everything was for sale and people were buying. There was nothing particularly blasphemous about this rampant materialism, but it seemed to ignite zeal for spiritual renewal among Evangelicals. Or was it just Cold War nerves and a fear of Russia and Communism, with firebrands like Wisconsin Senator Joe McCarthy barking like a junkyard dog about the "reds" who had infiltrated the government, the entertainment industry and dozens of other avenues of American life. Whatever the reasons, a wave of religious revivalism swept across America in the late 1940s. Billy Graham and his Youth for Christ movement attracted thousands to revival meetings that were broadcast across the land. Canada too caught the fever with religious programs from the People's Church in Toronto highlighted by Charles Templeton's spiritual pep talks.

He read about all this high-octane Christianity in the newspaper favoured by his father, *The Toronto Telegram,* and it was interesting enough, but he was content to pursue his own way to salvation with his internal narrative of living in Palestine in A.D. 30 and delivering his Sunday afternoon sermons to the bedposts. He read his Bible and waited for something dire to happen, often seeing only mischance and death around him: the red quarantine sign on the front door of a house where someone had diphtheria, the shrunken polio victim in his wheelchair, the newspaper account of a child's drowning in Georgian Bay in a summer storm. And always on the edge of his consciousness, the image of a boy leaning over too far and falling to his death in a dry well. Yet none of it mattered if you believed in Christ's promise of everlasting life.

But did he? Did he really believe in Christ's message, because as the months passed he sensed that his faith was faltering, especially when he was tempted by pleasure. Pleasure was sometimes irresistible. Take stealing for example. A violation of the Eighth Commandment. *Thou Shall Not Steal.* Clear as polished glass. Yet steal he did with his friend Gerald, a sly, clever boy a year older than him. The sheer thrill of getting something for nothing: a pencil box, a pack of playing cards, a chocolate bar slipped into his pocket while Gerald distracted the cashier. Gerald had many beguiling tricks up his sleeve. They were never caught.

He also found pleasure in the movies that he and Gerald watched on Saturday afternoons at the Capitol Theatre: the Laurel and Hardy shorts, the cartoons and the cowboy pictures. But his favourite movies were the melodramas, with their cops and bad guys and sultry-looking women. He went to these movies alone, sneaking into the theatre on Monday or Wednesday nights to watch Lana Turner inveigle an entranced John Garfield into murdering her husband in *The Postman Always Rings Twice*. His favourite actress was Barbara Stanwyck, and he watched her do the same to Fred MacMurray in *Double Indemnity*. He would never forget Stanwyck's determined walk down the stairs to confront and outwit the cocky insurance agent, the camera focusing solely on her legs and the anklet she wore, a scene that incited within him unsettling mysteries surrounding desire. The actress was featured on the poster in the theatre lobby, where she was described as *enticing*. The next day he looked up the word in a dictionary at the public library.

Entice: lure or attract by the offer of pleasure or reward.

How did he manage to see those movies on school nights! By lying to his mother, of course. A violation of the Ninth Commandment. *Thou Shalt Not Bear False Witness*. But he did. He told her he was at Gerald's working on homework. With no telephone yet in the house, his whereabouts could not be verified. But parents in small-town Ontario then were not unduly alarmed when children his age were out at night. And running through the dark streets after a free movie was pure elation. He was always home a few minutes before ten o'clock, when his mother was still listening to *Wayne and Shuster* or *Lux Radio Theatre*. His father would be in the basement waiting for the coal gas to burn off before going to bed. And that was another way to go if you weren't careful. Asphyxiated in your sleep. A dangerous world indeed.

Smart Alec

On other winter nights he walked across town with his father to the Arena Gardens to watch Intermediate Hockey with the Midland Flyers against the hated Collingwood Shipbuilders. They both stood for the games, leaning against the iron railing watching the players in their colourful sweaters race across the ice or slam one another against the boards. Sometimes there were fights both on the ice and in the stands. He would never forget those nights with his father watching hockey and then walking home through the quiet streets with only the sound of crunching snow beneath their feet and the creaking branches of the bare trees. These images would remain with him through all the years ahead, stored in his imagination for a novel about a hockey player and a bad marriage that would appear toward the end of that century. Its publication would dramatically change his luck.

Like thousands of other Canadian boys, he played shinny on

the town's streets. The term *road hockey* had not yet been invented and the game was played with a puck not a ball. They mostly used old sticks passed on by older brothers and worn down until the blades were scarcely half an inch in width. They called them toothpicks, and to stickhandle with such a weapon required the dexterity of a Max Bentley or a Rocket Richard. Going out the door after school to play often provoked a typical exchange between mother and son.

"You'll put your eye out with that thing. You mark my words."

"No, no, Ma. I'll put the other guy's eye out. He'll put mine out with his stick."

"Smart alec."

Their shinny games were sometimes watched by a large, simple man who lived with his parents. Elmer Chabot would stand on a snowbank at the side of the road observing the game in watchful silence. In the winters of the late forties there were still a few horse-drawn sleighs to be seen on the streets of his hometown, and so there were horse buns, which the boys cleared to the side of the road. For Elmer, these horse buns seemed to hold a particular fascination, and sooner or later he would step down from the snowbank and squatting inspect one until finally he would pick it up and stand holding it in his large mittened hand like an offering. One of the players would then have to remind him, "Don't eat that, Elmer, it's horseshit." And Elmer would carefully return it to the roadside. Elmer Chabot is long gone and so too are probably many of the boys he once played with on the streets of the town. But the boy carried that six-word directive with him for the rest of his life, a permanently relevant mantra, in the service of scorn for the promises of politicians and the blandishments of advertisers.

Early one morning during a fierce winter storm, he stood by the kitchen window watching his father make his way through the heavy drifts that blocked his path to the street. The snow was up to his hips, and he held his lunch pail aloft as he moved through the snow. Watching him, the boy decided that he owed his father a debt. His father supported them all; without him they would have no food to eat, no clothes to wear. He paid for the coal that he had to shovel into the furnace to keep them warm. Never once did he complain about any of this and that made it even more important to pay this debt. To show his father that he appreciated all this hard work, the boy decided that after the next snowfall he would surprise his father by clearing a way to the street so he wouldn't have to wear wet clothes before his workday began. The boy then listened to the weather forecasts on the radio, for winter storms were frequent in that part of the province, often sweeping down from Georgian Bay to engulf towns and countryside. And only a few days later he awakened in the dark to wind and falling snow.

Gathering his clothes he carried them past his sleeping brothers and made his way downstairs wearing the long underwear he slept in. The furnace was cooling and the floorboards were cold on his bare feet. In the kitchen he dressed hurriedly: his breeks and shirt and sweater; his boots and scarf. His woollen mitts and his aviator's cap with the big earflaps. The kitchen door led to a small porch at the back of the house and he had to push hard against the door to squeeze out into the snow and wind. He was now ready to repay his debt and so he began shovelling a passage toward the gateless wooden fence and the snowbanks on Ottawa Street. They had no car and his father had to walk to a neighbour's house for a ride. It was still dark but lights were coming on in the kitchen and upstairs windows as people prepared for the day. The kitchen light in his own house was now on and he saw his mother looking out, waving to him. But he was far too busy to wave back. His father would now be eating his breakfast, and he imagined his mother talking to his father about how his youngest son was out in the dark cold shovelling a path for him. Working steadily he felt grown-up and responsible, a serious boy at serious work. When his father came out the back door, the boy had almost reached the fence, a fine clear wide passage behind him from the back door. His father, bundled up in his winter jacket with the flaps of his work cap down against the wind, thanked him, and made his way to the gateless fence and then into the drifts of snow to Ottawa Street.

This happened again a week or so later, but this time when his father reached the fence he looked back and then pointed toward the street and smiled. His father told him then that he didn't like to criticize. He appreciated the effort, but perhaps the job could be done in a different way. Just shovel a narrow path to the road, he said. Just enough for him to get through. Then maybe he could finish the job after school. His father's suggestion made perfect sense. It was ridiculous to clear a path halfway to the street and then run out of time and watch his father wade through deep snow. He knew this, but each time he had hoped he could reach the road before his father came out of the house. And each time as he began, he could not resist the urge to widen the path before moving on. Somehow he felt compelled to do it this way.

Some years later he would be living in Toronto attending the Ryerson Institute of Technology, as it was then called, in the Radio and Television Arts program. By then he harboured a vague notion of using words to make his living. Would it be in radio or television plays? Or would it be words in a book? He was reading stories by Ernest Hemingway, admiring the spare, limpid prose. In the evenings he began his own stories, often imitating the famous American writer's style. But after writing an opening paragraph, he felt as he had on those dark winter mornings, compelled somehow to return to the opening sentence and begin a revision. It was as if he couldn't bear to leave the page in its unfinished state, and each evening he would return to the paragraph, reworking it by shifting words here and there, eliminating unnecessary modifiers, using stronger verbs. Trying to get it right. Or what he sensed might be *right*. It was all maddening, and by the end of the week he would be thoroughly fed up with this relentless revision of a paragraph that led nowhere, and evoked nothing. Whatever narrative energy the paragraph might have once possessed had now vanished. It would be a long time before he learned how to resist this compulsion to get everything right before moving on. And even then, when he began to write novels, he could write no more than twenty pages before returning to the beginning to revise. Then twenty more rough pages and it was time to widen the path.

One day in a bookshop on Bay Street he discovered *The Paris Review* and its interviews with famous writers. He was especially drawn to the sample pages of a writer's manuscript with its crossed-out words and the new words scribbled over them or in the margin. He always looked past the corrections to the original words, the author's first choice on a blank page, and he was often surprised by their banality. But it helped him to understand that a writer, even a famous writer, doesn't begin a story with a brilliant sentence. At least not on the first try. A blank page or screen always resists a brilliant opening sentence. There must first be other words and sentences, which can be edited or reworked, forgotten and replaced. His father was right about the path through the snow. You had to have a path. But it didn't have to be perfect. You could always revise it later. It was much the same with good writing. It was all about editing the words that had covered the blank page.

*

Sex was so mysterious to him then. It is difficult now in an age in which teenagers can find pornography at the touch of a computer keyboard to imagine how a thirteen-year-old-boy sixty years ago could know so little about sex. He knew the pleasure he could get from his own penis. Gerald had taught him that. But he couldn't yet understand how it worked with girls, even though Gerald had told him about inserting the penis into the vagina, a strange new word for the hole between a girl's legs. Gerald claimed to have "done it" many times with a cousin from Toronto who was visiting in the summer. He said they had taken long walks in Little Lake Park and found a "secret place to do it." The boy hated hearing such stories. Alone in the house he liked to snoop in drawers and once under a brother's sweater found a condom. On another day, looking through an old school desk in his parents' closet, he discovered two thin paperback books, a green one for females and a red one for males. Hoping to see pictures of men and women "doing it," he was instead frightened by gruesome photographs of male and female genitals marred with enormous lesions. There were pictures too of disfigured faces, some half eaten away by something called syphilis. He quickly put away these books, afraid they might cause nightmares.

Why, he wondered, would his parents have such books? He couldn't imagine either of them having such dreadful diseases. Who had brought them into the house to be finally hidden away and forgotten in a closet? When he thought about it, he decided that it must have been his father, who had a tendency to give in to people who sold things at the door. He himself had watched and listened as his father bought a Bible he would never read from two young Mormons in black suits. And then there was the elderly man who drove an ancient Dodge with a sign in one of the rear windows advertising various nostrums: WAMPOLE'S EXTRACT and DODD'S LITTLE KIDNEY PILLS and the hilariously alliterative LYDIA PINKHAM'S PINK PILLS FOR PALE PEOPLE. It had to be his father who was persuaded to buy the sex disease books from him. He knew that his mother was not to be trifled with at the front door, but his father seemed lightly armed against salesmen. The boy had once gone to the Canadian National Exhibition in Toronto with his father and watched him succumb to a man selling a small metal contraption shaped like a hen and designed to cut the top off a boiled egg. One could scarcely imagine a more useless appliance, yet his father had bought one for seventy-five cents. Why? the boy wondered. Did he feel sorry for the man who was reduced to such a pitiful livelihood? Why not just walk away as his mother would have done had she been there? "I'm not going to throw away good money on that," she might say. Was that not more sensible? Yet many years later, after his father's death, when the family was going through his personal effects, choosing what they would like as keepsakes, a ring, a watch, his service medals from the Great War, the writer rescued only the little metal hen.

With his sister in Toronto working at Eaton's and all three brothers now away on lake freighters, he had the bedroom to himself and his narrative fantasies. The house was quieter. His family, himself included, were by and large an opinionated, judgmental and quarrelsome lot. Equanimity was never a watchword for the household. It seemed to him that a streak of cussedness ran through both sides of his family, although his mother always blamed whatever shortcomings she encountered in her children on the Wrights.

"Your brother is just like Uncle so-and-so." Or "Your grandfather Wright was hard to live with. Everybody said so."

"Everybody, Ma? That's a lot of people."

"Never mind. It's the truth."

And perhaps it was.

Now and then his mother and father would quarrel, and soon a deep-freeze in the form of a prolonged silence would pass through the house. This might last for weeks, and sitting between them at supper he often felt misplaced and awkward. To tell the truth, he would have preferred to eat his meals alone sitting on the basement steps. Even then, at thirteen, he realized that it made no sense to sulk like that—two grown people unwilling to break the silence with so much as a "Pass the butter, you at the end of the table." No, it was, he decided, the wrong way to behave, yet ahead of him in the early years of his own marriage, he would pull the same stunt until his young, sensible wife told him in so many words that he should stop behaving like a child and say what was on his mind. It took a while, but he learned and for the rest of his life he was intrigued by what determined how we think and behave. Can we change what we see within ourselves and don't like? Is it possible to file down the sharp edges of a touchy and quarrelsome disposition? Can you overcome a tendency to impatience or jealousy? Or are such traits so hard-wired into our temperament they cannot be resisted?

Sometimes he wondered if his parents were happy together. Often they appeared to be, but sometimes not. Like everyone else, he supposed. And if it came to that, how many people were happy and for how long? Moments of happiness seemed to arrive unbidden and then depart. What prompted such feelings anyway? His father would never have talked about such matters, but his mother had no such compunction and, after one of these quarrels, she would sometimes turn to him when they were alone and fantasize about running away together. Just the two of them making their way in the world. This he couldn't understand. He listened to her and said nothing, but it bothered him. How would they live? he wondered. Where would they get money for food and clothes and shelter? He pictured them out on the street in the rain. Besides, he didn't want to leave the house on Fifth Street. He didn't want to leave his father and the rest of his family. Even though he sometimes didn't get along with his brothers, he still loved them. In time, of course, he would conclude that his mother's stories of running away were just stories; it was all a dramatization, a fantasy emerging from a part of her that insisted on complaining about her lot in life. He got used to listening to her without taking any of it seriously, and in fact his parents lived together for over fifty years. Like thousands of others in their time, they put up with things. They made do.

In elementary school he had been a good student, and this behaviour continued through his first year of high school. But in his second year he became indifferent to learning *anything*. Slouching in his seat at the back of the room, where the trouble-makers congregated, he exhibited almost no interest in what was going on, making only half-hearted attempts to complete assignments, daydreaming his way through the long afternoons, languorously defiant. To his teachers he was a "royal pain in the ass" and, when his history teacher said as much privately, he didn't mind a bit. After all, why object to the truth?

He may, in fact, have been suffering from a mild form of mononucleosis though he'd never heard of the disease and, as far as he could tell, neither had anyone else. No doctor was consulted, though in a way he yearned for some kind of sickness that might account for the lassitude he called "Monk's Torpor." When asked by classmates why he often fell asleep, he told them he had seen a doctor (a lie) and been diagnosed with a mild case of Monk's Torpor. When asked to explain, he said it was a disease named after an American, Dr. Henry Monk, who had discovered the malady during the Civil War, possibly to detect malingerers who were trying to evade battle duty. Where in the world had all that come from? Like his mother it seemed, he could easily inhabit a self-dramatizing world. Years later it came to him that during his first religious phase, at around age eleven or twelve, he may have read about Monk's Torpor in a book about monasteries in the Middle Ages. For a while he had fancied that one day he himself might become a monk. Monk's

Torpor, then, was just another name for acedia, an authentic ailment of monastic life:

Acedia: 1. onset of distaste for and boredom with all religious practices. 2. spiritual sloth or apathy, esp. that resulting from such an onset.

He remembered reading of how this could lead to despair and so victims were carefully monitored by abbots and other ecclesiastical worthies. His only gain from this farrago of contumacy and deception was the sympathy of an attractive classmate who had touched his arm and said how sorry she was for his sickness, but it was pointless for him to hope for anything more because she already had a boyfriend in grade twelve.

Shortly after school was out in June, he heard from a friend about a summer job at Lakeview Cemetery and he decided to apply. A cemetery. The perfect setting for the melancholy dreamer he imagined himself to be. The foreman of the work crew, which consisted of two elderly men, was a Scot named Duncan McKee, and his first question, "Are you the boy with the crippled hand?" so infuriated him that he wasn't at all certain that he wanted to work for the gruff old bugger.

Yet he was seized by a compulsion to show the man a thing or two. Or maybe even run him over. Without a word he walked to a wheelbarrow filled with dirt and wilted flowers and grasping the handles began to push the wheelbarrow in a large circle before stopping it in front of the old man. "Mr. McKee," he said, "unless you're looking for a piano player, I can do the job." He thought this display of bravado might send him packing. Instead Duncan McKee allowed himself a modest bark of laughter. "Well, all right. I suppose you can, son. You'll be working mostly with Alfred. That's him up there," and he pointed to a row of tombstones farther afield. All the boy could see was a shovel flinging dirt from a grave. "You'll be cutting grass and weeding the graves marked for Perpetual Care. But right now you'll be digging graves. We've got a baker's dozen of winter corpses in the basement of the chapel over there. We've got to get them underground by the end of the week before it gets too hot. Those folk died when the ground was too frozen to open."

He would be paid twenty-five dollars a week. He had never had twenty-five dollars in his life. As a weekly wage, it seemed like a small fortune, and in fact he enjoyed working at the cemetery, a serene and uncomplicated place with its trees and carefully cut grass, the flowers by the gravestones and the whirring of a sprinkler gently soaking the grass on a summer afternoon. He and Alfred worked hard that first week to dig the graves for the corpses in the chapel basement. He stood apart at the ceremonies when relatives and friends came to the funerals; leaning on his shovel, he was proud to be participating in the real work of preparing a resting place for the dead. Alfred Townsend was a lean tall man in his early sixties, a lifelong bachelor, it turned out, who had girlfriends, married women in their forties and fifties who were being *neglected* as Alfred put it by their husbands. Alfred was scrupulously fair about taking turns in "the hole" as he called the grave. But the physical work was invigorating, and though the boy was tired at the end of each day, he felt good about his body and his life. He loved the fresh air and the green grass and the fact that he was surrounded by the remains of hundreds of people who had once been living and breathing like himself. Now they were reduced to mouldering flesh and bone, just as one day he would be. In a way, he felt himself to be a part of something beyond his reach or understanding, and this proximity to the dead was oddly consoling. For the rest of his life he would enjoy walking in churchyards and cemeteries.

Duncan and Alfred went home for lunch, but he ate his sandwiches and his piece of cake or pie in the tool shed, reading library books: novels by John Steinbeck and Thomas Wolfe and Sinclair Lewis. That summer he read Sherwood Anderson's short stories in a book called *Winesburg, Ohio,* and the tales of small-town life seemed familiar to him. He also read *The Outline of History* by H. G. Wells and Erich Maria Remarque's *All Quiet on the Western Front.* Each Saturday afternoon he gave his mother five dollars. She didn't ask for it, but it pleased him to see how grateful she was. She had little money for personal use and so he was happy enough to keep her supplied with Ipana toothpaste and Italian Balm hand lotion and the odd package of Matinée cigarettes. The rest of his wages he saved, and by the end of the summer he had nearly two hundred dollars in the bank.

*

In his third year of high school a new English teacher, Mr. McCallister, appeared on the scene. He was young but confident, unperturbed by the rogues' gallery at the back of the room, enthusiastic though perhaps too full of himself to be likeable. Still his love for literature was infectious to a fifteen-year-old boy who had never confessed to anyone how much he loved words. The new teacher told them they would be studying *Macbeth* and Thornton Wilder's *Our Town* for the fall term. This news was predictably greeted by a collective groan. The year before they had read *Julius Caesar* on their own and then answered content questions which tested whether they had read the play or not. It was a boring exercise, and half the time many didn't know what was actually going on in the play. McCallister's plan, however, was to read the play in class and act out scenes, discussing them as they moved through the drama. After all, as he told them, Shakespeare's plays were written to be seen and heard in a theatre, adding that those in "the rear end" of the class would be perfect as the groundlings, burping and farting like their seventeenth-century counterparts. Following this there was much whispering. Did he actually say "burping and farting"? He had indeed, and you could say what you liked about it, but he had their attention and got a few laughs into the bargain.

The boy pretended not to care but he badly wanted to participate. He knew he could read well. As far as he was concerned, anyone who had read generous portions of the Bible could handle Shakespeare. But McCallister never looked his way. Why would he? He was part of the jeering mob at the back of the room. Not surprisingly the roles went to the ones who were labeled eager beavers, with their hands in the air waving frantically for attention. From the back of the room the groundlings squeaked in imitation of the girls, "Me please, sir, me please. Extra marks, sir." McCallister wisely ignored this nonsense and got on with his casting.

One day when his best student was absent and the readings themselves were teetering on the edge of collapse, McCallister assumed the role of Macbeth in the second scene of Act II when, following his murder of Duncan, Macbeth speaks to his wife about his guilt-laden insomnia.

Mac.—*Methought I heard a voice cry "Sleep no more!*
Macbeth doth murder sleep,"—the innocent sleep,
Sleep that knits up the ravell'd sleave of care,
The death of each day's life, sore labour's bath,
Balm of hurt minds, great nature's second course,
Chief nourisher in life's feast—

Lady—*What do you mean?*

Mac.—*Still it cried "Sleep no more!" to all the house;*
"Glamis hath murder'd sleep and therefore Cawdor
Shall sleep no more. Macbeth shall sleep no more!"

For a few moments he was *in* Duncan's castle overhearing this conversation and he felt . . . What did he feel? He couldn't say exactly—he knew only that something had happened within him as he listened to the words. The notion of sleep being murdered. A startling image, yet how apt. And the extraordinary metaphors for sleep itself; all of it leading to a powerful rhetorical picture of a man in deep distress.

The power of language to terrify or console. What else was there in moments of darkness but language? He was beginning to be dimly aware of this in McCallister's class on those long-ago autumn afternoons. There was pleasure in appreciating a well-written line or sentence. His attitude was changing. McCallister may have been a conceited little twit, but he was a damn good teacher, and the boy began to pay more attention, listening to the words of Shakespeare as they were spoken, noting McCallister's suggestions. "Not quite, Linda. Listen, she is puzzled by her husband. After the murder he's changed. He's not the man she used to know. Lady Macbeth is impatient with her husband's strange behaviour and you must show that in your voice. Pay attention to the words Shakespeare gives you to read." Yes, thought the boy, pay attention to the words. They are all we have.

In the second half of the term they read Thornton Wilder's *Our Town*, a touching if sentimental portrait of a small New England town at the beginning of the twentieth century. To his astonishment McCallister asked him to read the part of sixteen-year-old George, son of the local doctor, who is in love with Emily Webb, the daughter of the town's newspaper publisher. He took the play home and reread it the night before, trying to decide how he would approach the role, worried sick that he would make a hash of it. In fact, the next day he did very well and, though McCallister said nothing, he smiled at him as if claiming this small victory over loutish ignorance. As for himself, he tried not to seem too pleased though he was elated. Best of all, some of the girls now looked at him differently. Was it curiosity or admiration or both? Two or three congratulated him. One of them said, "I forgot I was in the classroom when you read." Truth or flattery? Or both? The back row boys said nothing, but he knew his participation was viewed as betrayal. He had gone over to the other side, one of the few triumphs in another lacklustre year that saw him continue to fumble his way toward grade twelve. As usual, math remained the stumbling block. He had to have at least one math credit, but he couldn't pass grade eleven geometry. Those angles and triangles and parallelograms meant nothing to him. He wrote about it. Asked to write a *persuasive essay* on a subject of his choice, he entitled his attempt "Euclid to Thee I Bow, Not in Admiration but Confusion." An unwieldy title no doubt, but the essay at least expressed his frustration. McCallister's verdict was not unsympathetic, though doubtless accurate. *Excellent word choice, but poorly argued. 65%.*

The Wright family at Christmas 1953.
The author, age sixteen, is seated behind his mother.

In the 1950s only a handful of high-school graduates went on to university to become doctors, engineers, lawyers, architects, clergymen or high-school teachers. The group below them settled for the grade twelve junior matriculation, which enabled them to enroll in nursing programs, business colleges for secretarial work, elementary-school teaching and so on. The rest of the school population often left after two or three years, content to find work locally on lake freighters like his brothers, or in small factories. Some worked for the town and others on Main Street in clothing or grocery stores or as mechanics in garages. By now he had a vague notion of earning a livelihood by writing. But how? During the last year of high school, he discovered J. D. Salinger's *The Catcher in the Rye*, a timeless look at a young outsider who won't or can't fit in to the world around him. He can still remember the red deerstalker cap on the cover of the paperback, but how he came by the book will forever be a mystery, for there were no bookstores worth the name in the town.

But there was now television, black and white and technologically primitive compared to sixty years later, but there just the same in living rooms across the country. And in spite of his fascination with words on a page, he was intrigued by the new medium. As his father once said, "Imagine that! Picture shows in the living room!" They only got one station, CKVR in Barrie, Ontario, and programming didn't begin until the six o'clock news. In the early days when his father came home from work, they sat together for half an hour looking at the Indian Head test pattern while waiting for supper and the six o'clock news. Yes, there on the screen in the living room was only the picture of a test pattern, but in those early days it still produced a kind of wonder.

What he really waited for, however, were the plays broadcast in the evenings live before a studio audience. Sponsored by corporate America, programs like *Kraft Theatre*, the *United States Steel Hour* and Westinghouse's *Studio One* reached millions of living rooms. The CBC carried some of these shows and also had its own *General Motors Presents*. Writing for television, he thought, must be impossibly glamorous and sexy. But how did you get that kind of job? It was 1954 and he was seventeen years old, and soon he would have other things on his mind. In the last week of school, in the midst of writing examinations for his junior matriculation, he was in a bad car accident.

A sunny June Saturday afternoon and he and two friends were cruising Little Lake Park in Tommy's fire-engine-red hot rod, a 1932 Ford with a '36 V-8 engine, the three of them, checking out the "hair pie" as Bert called it. Along the beach the girls walked or lay on the grass verge in their bathing suits. A beep on the horn then to alert the little beauties that they were being admired by three cool dudes in the hottest car in town. A few smiled and waved, but one turned her backside to them and pointed at it. He stood up in the moving car to cry out, "Why, you hussy! Showing us your bum like that." Laughter on both sides. Still the smart alec. All good fun on a summer day and all about to change for him.

A few minutes later they were on King Street turning left onto Yonge en route to Balm Beach and more ogling. Tom was careful about staying within the speed limit, for the garish little car was a target for the cops. He would open up the Ford once they were beyond the town limits. They were approaching Eighth Street near the Dairy Queen and the Parkside Pavilion, where his brothers sometimes danced with girlfriends on Saturday nights and his sister had once sung with a local band. Ahead of him he could see the car, a big heavy late forties Oldsmobile waiting at the entrance to the park. Bert knew the driver, a guy in his twenties living on Eighth Street. He was waiting to turn right onto the highway and then left onto Eighth Street. But first he had to let them pass. Instead he chose to come out and then cross the highway in front of them at Eighth Street. But he must have misjudged their speed and so, just as Bert whispered "Christ, watch out," Tom hit the brakes, but it was too late. The big car struck them head-on and he was pitched forward, his face hitting the old steel dashboard.

He staggered from the car, his mouth full of blood and pieces of his front teeth, his nose smarting and surely broken. He let a girl coming out of the Dairy Queen help him to a bench near the entrance to the restaurant, where he stared dully at the wreckage of the two cars in the middle of the highway. Tom and the other driver were talking loudly and angrily. He could hear a siren. Well, at least he was alive; he could easily have been tossed from that little car if they'd been going a bit faster. He decided then that this was the only way to look at matters. He had survived the collision. He was alive. Oddly enough his two friends were unmarked. Cars were now slowing down to have a look. He had seen people doing that before and in fact he had done so himself. Passing a wreck is a moment of happiness in spite of what people might think. You pass an accident and you may cluck in sympathy for the victims, but deep down inside you are really saying, "Better him than me." Or so he always thought. When the girl from the Dairy Queen asked him if he was okay, he said, "No, I'm not okay. I'm still alive, but as you can see I'm definitely not okay."

Someone took him to the hospital, where he was patched up, and someone else put him in a taxi and he arrived home just as the family was finishing supper. By now his eyes were blackened, and when he opened the door his mother saw him and shrieked. "My God, you have been in an accident."

"It's not as bad as it looks, Ma."

"Your teeth. Your beautiful teeth!"

"Yeah, well. I'll get some new ones. Teeth are replaceable."

One of his brothers was home then from the lakes. "I told you so, didn't I?" he said. "I told you that sooner or later you were going to get into trouble in that damn car."

I told you so. Four words arranged into what is probably the most useless sentence in the English language. Or any language for that matter. Always delivered *after* an unhappy event foretold by the teller. *I told you so* serves no purpose beyond offering a shaky confirmation of the teller's prescience, a way of saying yet again "I was right." Not a helpful utterance, then, but for some, apparently an irresistible one.

His mother was in tears and he was sorry about that, but there was nothing to be done but reassure her that what was broken could be mended. At such times platitudes work best.

Away from the clamour of his excitable family he examined his face in the bathroom mirror behind a closed door. He looked as if he'd just gone ten rounds with Sugar Ray Robinson. At the end of the fight they had embraced in the middle of the ring.

"Good fight, kid. You did okay."

"Thanks, Champ. The best experience of my life so far."

They touched gloves. A moment to cherish and his manager agreed. "You couldn't get past his left jab, kid. He was nailing you all through the fight with that left jab."

"I know, Whitey. He was just too fast for me."

"Hey, he's the best in the world. Ten rounds with Sugarman

and you were still on your feet when the bell rang. That's something to tell your grandkids."

It was the beginning of a weird summer, but somehow he managed to pass the matriculation exams. The graveyard job was gone. By the time he applied he was too late. Duncan McKee was sorry but he'd needed someone weeks before. Again they'd had corpses in the chapel basement and had to get them underground before they turned in the hot weather. He understood. But there were no other jobs in sight and so he spent his afternoons talking to girls in the park. They would ask him how he was feeling and touch his face. When he winced, they would say how sorry they were. His girlfriend, a former cheerleader and a local beauty whom he had been trying unsuccessfully to seduce for a full year, was also sympathetic to his plight. But not that sympathetic. Not in 1954, before birth control pills. A smart girl.

Tobacco Road

In time his wounds healed and after some tricky and expensive dental work he was whole again and reading the American writer Erskine Caldwell's *God's Little Acre* and *Tobacco Road,* two paperbacks he'd found (snooping again) in the pockets of a winter coat in his mother's closet, of all places. Caldwell's novels had enjoyed a mild notoriety in the 1930s for their louche depiction of country life in the southern United States. Where in the world had his mother found those books? Yet when he thought of it, she'd always had a sly fascination with the shady side of life, especially attracted to movies about gangsters. He could remember going with her on Wednesday nights to the Capitol Theatre to see films like *Folsom Prison, City Across the River, Knock on Any Door* with Humphrey Bogart. But why not? As for Erskine Caldwell, the seventeen-year-old literary critic wasn't particularly drawn to his prose nor did he find the sex scenes all that beguiling. Yet for some reason he liked the title

Tobacco Road, and so when his friend Mel suggested they try to find work in the tobacco fields of southwestern Ontario, he agreed. He saw it as an adventure and a chance to make some real money. Tobacco picking he'd heard paid well.

On a Monday morning in early August, they set forth, hitch-hiking along Ontario highways, picked up by everyone from Korean War veterans with their stories to doleful middle-aged men with their inevitable caches of filthy black and white snap-shots in the glovebox, which the boys dutifully examined to keep the old perverts happy. Astonishing what people got up to, he thought as he looked at a middle-aged woman with pendu-lous breasts. She was on her hands and knees being serviced by a Great Dane. Far from inflaming him, the picture put him in mind of a popular song of the early fifties, "How Much Is That Doggie in the Window?" He began to laugh and wouldn't or couldn't stop until the flummoxed driver pulled over and or-dered them out of the car in the middle of nowhere.

They slept overnight in a cemetery on the outskirts of St. Thomas, where a poster read TOBACCO PICKERS WANTED. EXPERIENCE HELPFUL, BUT NOT NECESSARY. The next day they were hired by a farmer who seemed to like Mel, but took an instant dislike to him. The farmer had noticed his left hand, and, though he didn't say anything about it, he may have felt he was taking on a liability. The work was hard and dirty. It was stoop labour in the heat of August, and at the end of the day they were tired with aching backs. Their fellow workers were mostly older, many from Quebec. They drank beer in the evenings and often quarrelled among themselves. The bunkhouse stank of cigarette smoke and dirty feet. At night he lay listening to most of them jacking off in the darkness. Sometimes he walked by a small river to get away from it all; he missed his girlfriend and wrote letters to her describing his life on the farm and his loneliness and longing for her. Sometimes he sat by the river's edge and watched the evening sky, singing jukebox hits of the day.

One morning at breakfast in the farmhouse, the farmer's wife, who was pretty and at least ten years younger than her husband, told the boy she had heard him singing and thought he was good enough to be on the radio. It was a well-intentioned but mortifying observation to make in front of a tableful of transient farm workers slurping their porridge and tearing their toast. He knew he would pay for it and he did; in the rows that morning a falsetto voice was heard from among the tobacco pickers, "Sing me a song, hoochie coochie man." Another would try a horrible rendition of Roy Hamilton's hit, "You'll Never Walk Alone." The mockery was relentless and the farmer was the worst offender. The youth began to count the hours until Labour Day, when he and Mel agreed they would leave. Meantime, flaked out on his cot in the bunkhouse, he listened to the inventive profanity of the arguments that smouldered around him until they burst finally into fist fights. In the morning the combatants would be gone.

He took to the bank of the little river with his pencil and steno pad and began a story about a seventeen-year-old boy who remarkably enough resembled himself working on a tobacco farm for a man who clearly disliked and tormented him with his jibes about reading poetry. But the farmer's young wife had fallen for the boy and would meet him late at night in the fields, with a blanket on which they lay. She taught him how to love her and soon their rapturous cries carried across the fields. The farmer, of course, discovered this infamy and murdered the boy with a hatchet. Then, in sorrow and anger, the farmer's wife killed her husband with an old handgun she found in the attic. Only two bullets remained, but it was enough. With the last one, she killed herself. He thought it might make a good play for television. But then he read it a few days later and thought otherwise. The narrative pattern reminded him too much of a nursery rhyme from his childhood,

> *This is the maiden all forlorn*
> *That milked the cow with the crumpled horn*
> *That tossed the dog*
> *That worried the cat*
> *That killed the rat*
> *That ate the malt*
> *That lived in the house that Jack built.*

To his surprise, a few days later Mel said he'd had enough and was leaving that afternoon. How thrilling that announcement was! It was Mel who had given in, not himself. He remembered standing up in the row and looking around. In another few hours he would be free of this place.

In the last year of high school he was finally relieved of the burden of his virginity by Veronica, a freewheeling spirit who had grown up in Penetang but was attending high school in Midland. She was a deeply sensual girl with plenty of experience at nineteen and to his amazement told him that she'd had a crush on him from the first day of school. She also had use of her father's car, the favourite trysting place of all teenagers, and, in the spacious back seat of that old Chrysler, she taught him how to love her. That year he had applied to Ryerson Institute of Technology, as it was known in those days, and he was accepted into the Radio and Television Arts program. A modest insurance settlement from the car accident would pay his way through the first year. He and Veronica would enjoy one another on weekends in Toronto for the next several months and then drift apart.

Toronto in the 1950s has often been portrayed as a stuffy reminder of propriety and Protestant rectitude, a city of churches where on Sunday you couldn't go to a movie or buy a glass of beer. And, he supposed, it *was* stodgy and provincial if you compared it to, say, New York or Chicago or San Francisco, but perhaps it was not all that different from, say, Minneapolis or Leeds. Coming from a Georgian Bay town of six thousand, he found "the city," as people up there called it, exciting with its new subway and neon-lit Yonge Street. In 1956, it was filled with immigrants who had fled a ravaged Europe and were looking to find their way in a new world: Poles and Czechs, Hungarians, Latvians and Estonians, Italians. Some referred to them derisively as DPs, short form for displaced persons. He shared a basement apartment in a house on Sorauren Avenue near Queen Street in the west end, and he saw the men in their long leather coats and the women with bandanas on their heads walking along Roncesvalles Avenue. There were no beggars, no homeless people. Just folks looking for work and often finding it in factories like Massey-Harris and Kodak. They worked hard, saved their money and planned for a more prosperous future for their children. Some opened second-hand clothing stores or lunch counters.

Each weekday morning he boarded an eastbound streetcar at McGill Street and watched these people, strangers in a new land, struggling with a new language. How difficult it must be for them, he thought. Getting off at Yonge Street he walked north to Shuter and then east past Massey Hall, where he had once listened to Jazz at the Philharmonic, and north again a few blocks to Ryerson, tucked in behind Yonge Street, bounded by Gerrard to the north and Dundas to the south and Church on the east. Only a few years before it had been an RCAF training centre, and some of the classes were still held in Quonset huts. He wanted to write for television, or so he thought, and went about attending classes in everything from radio announcing to television production. He found a lifelong friend in Mike, a big amiable former high school football star who had visions of being a sportscaster. Looking back on his Ryerson days, he seems to remember only that the two of them spent most of their time that first year playing snooker in a pool hall on the northwest corner of Yonge and Gould. You went up the stairs to a smoky room, leaving your cares and assignments behind you. Across Yonge Street was Steele's Tavern, a favourite hangout of Ryerson students where you could generally get served without too much fuss over how old you were. The legal drinking age then was twenty-one. He was nineteen, but, looking like a sixteen-year-old, he always chose dark corners.

The course work at Ryerson was interesting enough and the teachers were fine, but by his second year he was cultivating old bad habits from his high-school days. Slouched in his seat during lessons, doodling with story ideas. Taking entire afternoons off for snooker and beer or sitting in the library reading novels and short stories. What was he reading then? He can only remember Somerset Maugham's *The Razor's Edge,* though he must have read a hundred other books. At times he wondered if he should have taken journalism. Didn't journalism have more affinity with real writing than radio and television arts? Hadn't old Hem once worked as a reporter with the *Toronto Star?* He was beginning to have doubts about the veracity and worth of television dramas. How formulaic even some of the best ones were! There was little complexity in the characters. No ambiguity. Nothing to upset the corporate sponsors. It was all about simplicity and happy endings. How realistic was that? How many happy endings were there in life? None. Sooner or later we all ended up dead.

By his final year he was dismayed by all his uncertainty. A low tolerance for uncertainty is a recipe for anxiety, and he was anxious. He was now twenty-two and in another six weeks would be graduating. Where would he go? What would he do to earn his living? How did you start a career in advertising or broadcasting or television? Already some of his classmates had lined up jobs at the CBC or CTV as radio operators or television cameramen. The silkier voiced were headed for announcing and disc jockey jobs in radio stations across the country. There didn't seem to be any openings for wannabe writers. In desperation he sent out letters to advertising agencies offering his meager talents, pleading for a chance to get a foothold in the business. He received only one reply, a telephone call from one Harry Painter, who spoke with what sounded like an American accent. His voice was like something he might have heard on radio. "How about lunch?" asked Painter, and rather boldly he invited the adman to the Savarin on Bay Street. His funds were low and the place was a little pricey, but he had to make a good impression.

A few days later he climbed the stairs to the restaurant, where the maître d' took him to Painter's table. Apparently his guest was well known at the Savarin. Harry Painter was a small man, perhaps in his fifties, impeccably dressed in a dark blue suit, white shirt with a narrow maroon tie and a white handkerchief in the upper pocket of his suit coat. Yet despite the nifty Madison Avenue threads, there was a haggard look about him, an edgy nervousness in his manner.

"What are you drinking, kid?" he asked. "I usually have a martini or two with lunch."

There was already an empty cocktail glass in front of him. But the young man was thinking about the bill. He had forty dollars in his wallet, but with Painter sinking martinis, the reckoning could be worrisome. He asked for a beer, but Painter interrupted. "Bring the young man a martini and another for me." Painter smiled. "If you're thinking seriously of advertising, kid, don't drink beer. It sends the wrong message. What do they call you? Richard? Or Dick?"

In fact for most of his life he had been called Bruce, a name he had loathed since childhood, when friendly neighbours or visiting relatives would pat his little blond head and call him Brucie. It always made him want to swear or stick out his tongue, though he never did. He had been christened Richard Bruce and much preferred his first name, so as soon as he left Midland he called himself Richard or Dick, new handles for a new life.

"Well, Dick it is then," said Painter as the waiter served their drinks. Painter did not seem to be interested in ordering food but talked instead about his days in television. He mentioned *Philco Playhouse*, a program he once worked on in New York. Painter said he was from New York. The young man thought about the list of questions he had written on a piece of paper in his pocket, but sensed that it might be considered gauche to present the list. Thinking about the questions may have caused his mind to wander a little because he seemed to be listening to a man so embittered by his experience in television that he was now in the midst of a sudden withering condemnation of the medium. It was as if the sole purpose of the lunch was not to offer advice on how to get into the business, but actively to discourage him from going anywhere near it. "Dick," Painter said, leaning forward and just in time to avoid knocking over his finished martini glass, "if I were you, I would run as fast as I could in the other direction. Find some worthy labour elsewhere. A schoolteacher maybe or a librarian. You've said you like books. Well that's great, but nobody in TV admits to liking books. Writing for the box is a mug's game. I speak from experience or I wouldn't be here talking to you today." He instantly caught the passing waiter's attention with only two fingers in the air. "It's a nasty business," he continued, "filled with people who don't stab you in the back. They slip the blade between your ribs while they're smiling at you." He looked away as if remembering a particularly painful encounter between a knife blade and his rib cage. He shook his head, "I should have been a cantor," he said. "I had the voice. My mother begged me. On her hands and knees in the kitchen. Go to the synagogue, Harry. Make a life for yourself there. God has given you a gift."

"Like Al Jolson," the young man said, remembering *The Jolson Story* and *Jolson Sings Again*. He told Harry Painter of seeing those movies with his mother when he was ten or eleven. Walking together downtown through a summer evening with the smell of cut grass. The seven o'clock show at the Capitol Theatre with its wooden seats. He stopped, and to his surprise

Painter said, "Christ, that's wonderful, Dick. I'll bet you can't remember who played Jolson in those movies."

"Larry Parks," he said. "At one time he was blacklisted by the Commie hunters. Senator McCarthy's gang."

"Good for you," said Painter. "You're too fucking smart to go into television. Let's have another."

"I'm getting a little hungry, Harry. Maybe we should eat."

"Eat, schmeet. There's a time to eat and a time to drink."

"And a time to gather stones together."

"What?"

"Ecclesiastes. I used to be a preacher in my own mind. Read the Bible. Even the Old Testament."

"No shit?"

"No shit. Leviticus and Deuteronomy were struggles. I was only eleven."

"Who would have thought? A nice Christian boy reading the Pentateuch. Where were you brought up anyway?"

"In a burg up the highway ninety miles from here. Georgian Bay area."

"Even so," Painter said and left it there while the waiter brought another round of gin and vermouth. The young man was having trouble navigating his way back to the original purpose of the lunch with this stranger. Did it not have something to do with future employment? A hint or two of how to get a foothold in advertising or television? But either to his dismay or to his relief, he was growing more and more convinced that neither pathway was for him. Yet teaching didn't particularly appeal. Forty years of standing in front of a blackboard instructing kids on the difference between a gerund and a participle. "Maybe I'll write a novel," he said. The words had come out of his mouth unbidden; it was the first time he had said them to another human, and once spoken they sounded preposterous. Write a novel? What a thing to say at his age! His words were what a friend referred to as "drunken utterance" and as such were not to be taken seriously. He hoped that Harry was also now too tight to have heard. But had he then just burned up three years of instruction in radio and television arts for nothing? And how the hell was he going to pay for all the martinis they were drinking? Plus the meal yet to come. The management would likely call the police. Oddly enough, or perhaps not oddly, he no longer cared. But Harry had been listening. Indeed he had and he looked a little . . . What was the word? *Wistful* perhaps?

"I wrote a novel once," he said. "It made the rounds of publishers in New York, but it kept coming back. You may be a little young to contemplate such an ambition." He allowed himself a sigh as if life's misfortunes were giving him pause. He finished his latest martini in two swallows and seemed to perk up. "Well, I suppose you can contemplate writing one at your age, but actually getting down to doing it comes later, when you want revenge on all the pricks who made your life so difficult." He thought for a moment and then added, "Yes. The impulse usually arrives when you've wended your way through this wearisome voyage we call life."

"Harry," he said, "if you wrote like that, I'm not surprised those publishers turned down your novel."

"I like you, Dick. It is Dick, isn't it?"

"Yes it is, but I prefer Richard. Dick has some risible connotations."

"You've got a way with words, Richard. I'd hate to see you

waste it on some crappy TV show or use it to write jingles for laxatives. I'd hate to see you go astray."

"Astray," he said. His head was beginning to hurt. There was now another martini in front of him. "Astray," he said again. "A word you don't often hear in conversation. A word for a poet. I like the sound of that word, Harry."

Harry didn't appear to be listening. "I just want you to remember, Dick, that you're going to hit some bumps along the road. Everybody does. But you'll find your way. There will be bumps but you'll find your way. Just keep in mind that life is not all cock and pickles."

"Sage advice, Harry," he said. "Words to live by." He finished his third martini. Or was that his fourth?

Christ, he was drunk! Had he ever been so hammered in his life? Had he climbed stairs to this restaurant? He thought about it. Yes, there were stairs somewhere and he could dimly remember climbing them. But how in the world would he get *down* the stairs? He had serious doubts about whether he could even walk on a level surface. But Harry Painter was again shaking his head. "Jesus, Larry Parks. *The Jolson Story*. Dick, tell me again about walking to the movies with your mother on those summer evenings, the light falling through the leaves of the trees."

He couldn't remember much of what he'd said. He had invented most of it. Yes, he and his mother had gone to the movies together, but it might have been an evening in the spring or in the autumn. He certainly couldn't remember any light falling through the leaves, though he supposed it must have been doing that. What he had done was invent the scene, in the service of what? He tried to think. A long word that began with the letter *v*. After a while it emerged from his alcohol-soaked brain. *Verisimilitude.*

Harry was gazing into his empty glass. "What was that, Richard?"

"Nothing," he said. But it wasn't nothing. It was something. He had told some lies to arrive at a kind of truth. The stock-in-trade of a novelist, though perhaps he didn't quite realize it at the time. Although some of what he'd described hadn't actually happened, its inclusion had enriched the scene for Harry Painter.

They finally ordered food. He had given up worrying about the bill. If not arrested, he would resign himself to washing dishes for the next three days. Harry ordered a steak, while he settled for a ham sandwich. After the waiter left, Harry said, "I'm looking after all this, by the way. I've really enjoyed talking to you, Dick. It's been worth every penny."

He can still remember how he very nearly fell on those stairs. Harry had gripped his arm and guided him down the steps to the street and put him in a taxi. They promised to meet again soon. But as the weeks went by he forgot, until just before he left Toronto, when he phoned the ad agency and asked for Harry Painter. A female voice told him that Harry had "passed away" several weeks before. When he went to the public library and looked up the obituary, he found that Harry had died suddenly, leaving only a sister in California. He was sixty-two. Was it a heart attack? A stroke? Cancer? Cirrhosis? The obituary didn't say.

*

Late in August of 1959 he was working at a public bath down-town as a lifeguard in the swimming pool and general dogsbody, mopping the floor and cleaning the stalls on the men's side of the bathhouse. This summer job was about to expire. For the past two years he had been living in the apartment on the second floor of the building with his girlfriend Maxine and her mother, who also worked at the bathhouse. He had his own room, but he and Maxine found time and space for an intense love affair, often swimming together naked at night in the pool. He was buying Ramses by the dozens to stave off fatherhood and its obvious complications. But the affair was drawing to a close. He wanted desperately to get started on something approaching a career and, having found nothing in either advertising or television, he decided to try his luck in journalism. With no experience or academic credentials, it would not be easy, but he fastened his hope on the notion of finding some hardbitten old editor who would appreciate an industrious young man with no qualifications beyond curiosity and a love of language. They could have him cheaply too. In the time-honoured tradition of sons who have yet to find their way, he returned to his parents' home, and a small desk in the old bedroom he once shared with his three brothers. There he began pecking out a letter on his portable Smith-Corona. It wouldn't do, he thought, to send out carbon copies, and so he typed the letter forty-nine more times on the little machine. Fifty letters to fifty papers across the province, mostly to weeklies or small-city dailies. He knew he wouldn't stand a chance with the big newspapers in places like Toronto and Hamilton and Ottawa.

He received two replies to the fifty letters, one in striking cal-ligraphy from Robertson Davies, then editor of *The Peterborough*

Examiner, who had no openings but wished him well in his pursuit of employment. Fifteen years later, at a symposium at Trent University to celebrate the novelist Margaret Laurence, he would have the opportunity to thank Davies in person for his thoughtfulness in replying to the letter of a very green young man. Davies, a Victorian presence in cape and beard, smiled gravely but understandably could not recall the particulars. By then they had both published recent novels.

The other reply came from the owner of a small weekly in the Caledon Hills, north of Toronto, who asked to see him. After the interview he was hired as a reporter and yet again a dogsbody (from time to time he was asked to pick up dry cleaning or fetch certain items from the local hardware store for the owner's wife). His salary was thirty-five dollars a week. Until he could find a place that wouldn't absorb too much of that, he slept in the owner's basement on an ancient davenport, attending to his grooming needs at the sink by the washing machine, taking his meals in a grease pit on the main street of the hamlet, reminding himself that experience was everything. These arrangements would do for now. Or so he thought. Soon he was covering "the local scene" as the owner called it, with its council meetings and church suppers. To get around he was given the use of a ten-year-old Ford with a balky clutch, each takeoff commencing with starts and stops, an overall jerkiness that caused considerable mirth among onlookers, much like Monsieur Hulot in the French farce *Mr. Hulot's Holiday.*

One day in late September he was assigned the task of interviewing a local farmer whose sow Doris had won first prize at an agricultural exhibition. The man was exuberant with pride and eagerly escorted him to the barn, where they stood together admiring Doris, an enormous creature snorting and grunting and farting in her pen, the bright crimson ribbon still around her neck. He took notes on the animal's diet and disposition, daring to ask if she was in line for motherhood. The good-natured farmer said that indeed she was, and they both enjoyed a chuckle, which for him might well have been a prelude to sobbing, as he foresaw years of interviewing people with weird hobbies. On his way back to town he pulled off the road by a cemetery. There was nothing like a cemetery to settle his nerves and offer perspective. Sitting with his back against a tombstone, he considered his situation. His living conditions between the washtubs and the lines of drying underwear were nothing to look forward to at the end of the day. Yet finding a room or small apartment meant committing himself to a long winter of covering local curling tournaments. What did he know about curling? Nothing. But after nearly three weeks, the owner's wife too was growing impatient; more than once he listened to her complaints drifting down from above. "When is he going to find his own place? It's a nuisance to have a stranger in your basement." True enough, he thought. He *was* a nuisance, passing to and fro on his way out, interrupting the flow of everyday routine, and to no good purpose. He was an excrescence, a bunion on the foot of the household. Like Perkins's chickens, which had so bedeviled his poor mother.

That week he was rereading Albert Camus's *The Outsider*, and he had brought the book with him to the cemetery, where he sat reading once again the final pages of the novel. How he admired the calm and steady voice of the narrator, Meursault, his courage and truthfulness as he recounts how he came to be in prison awaiting execution. The voice from faraway North

Africa, and yet how appealing to him as he sat in a cemetery on the edge of a cornfield in Ontario on a late-summer afternoon listening to the crows in the branches of the maple trees, watching the slanting sunlight and the dust raised from a car passing along the country road, hearing the faint sound of a farm machine, reading the inscription on the tombstone in front of him. He was trying to take it all in, sitting there on top of the dead. He would think about that afternoon many times in the future, though never more so than only a few months later when he read in a newspaper of the death of Camus, killed in a road accident in France. He was only in his forties.

Some luck then in his life. A week or so after his visit to Doris, he was given his marching orders by the owner's wife; this was on a Friday and he had to be out of her basement by Monday. When he called his mother to expect him for the weekend, she said there was a letter awaiting him from a radio station in Orillia. When he had sent out his fifty letters, he had listed his parents' address for replies. Was it a job offer, he wondered, or just condolatory words from a kind-hearted editor? It didn't matter. He had to go. If he stayed in that hamlet, he foresaw only a future of interviewing the couple who went to England on an ocean liner, or the gardener with the largest squash at the fall fair, the jigsaw fanatic, the hundred-year-old man who still curled. He saw himself in ten years, with greying hair, a dyspeptic and despairing alcoholic. The owner was decent enough about his abrupt departure and paid him his final thirty-five dollars. By Monday noon he was on a bus with his one suitcase and a bag of books.

The next day he had an interview with the manager of the radio station in Orillia. They needed a continuity writer, and his letter had been forwarded by the editor of the newspaper, a fellow Rotarian who thought the applicant's qualifications more suited to radio than to newspapers. This was true enough, and by the following Monday he was working for CFOR, the Voice of Central Ontario, writing copy for local merchants and car dealers, highlighting sales on men's apparel at a haberdashery or the weekend specials at the A&P. Each day he wrote obituaries for a funeral home and after the newscast at noon listened to his words solemnly announced over a recording of Handel's Largo.

That fall and winter his loneliness was assuaged by literature and sex. From the public library he borrowed books by the armful, novels and story collections by Joseph Conrad and Graham Greene, William Faulkner and F. Scott Fitzgerald. He read Joyce's *A Portrait of the Artist as a Young Man* twice and the stories in *Dubliners*, studying the sentences to see how they carried the words. Could anyone, he thought, write a better short story than "The Dead"?

On Saturday nights he had sex with a waitress who worked in one of the restaurants where he often ate dinner, always alone and with a book. Her name was Donna, and she seemed drawn to or puzzled by his solitude and his absorption in books. She was eighteen, a tall pale girl with a plain face and an awkward laugh, as if unsure that a sarcastic remark had been hurtful or funny or neither; a girl who wanted to please, but didn't know how. He can no longer remember how they came to be lovers; perhaps it was as simple as both of them being in need of company. On Saturday nights she babysat three young children in a house on Atherley Road, a long walk on winter nights. The children's parents were drinkers and went to the Atherley Arms on the outskirts of town, and they didn't return until after midnight, when they were usually drunk but still good-natured. They didn't appear to mind his presence there on the couch.

But earlier, after they left for those evenings, Donna was careful about everything. Once the children were asleep she closed the blinds on the front window and turned off all the lights except one table lamp. She would then insist that he undress them both. The first time he saw her naked he was astounded at the beauty of her body. He would never have guessed that beneath the dowdy uniform she wore in the restaurant was perfection. From that first night he praised it endlessly, and the words seemed to excite her. She would cling to him, whispering hoarsely, "Tell me again, say it again. Don't stop. Say it again." And so he would praise her feet and thighs, her throat, her perfect breasts. Words in service to Eros.

Beyond the sex they never had much to say to one another. Donna had no interest in his background or even what he did for a living. When he told her he worked at the radio station, she didn't ask what he did and he didn't tell her. She offered only glimpses of herself and her life with an alcoholic mother in a wheelchair (road accident), a father she didn't even remember, a sister in Kingston who was living common law with a "prick." But she didn't dwell on anything. When he once asked what she would like to do in her life, she became annoyed and asked him what he meant, and he began to sense that there was something unreachable about the girl, some deep-seated resistance to any intimate disclosure. He sensed too an anger within her, a rage just waiting to burst forth. He didn't think he wanted to be around when it happened.

A winter of worry and frustration then with his library books and his feral girlfriend. You could call her a girlfriend, he supposed, but she was really only a sex partner. They shared no stories of each other's lives; they confided nothing and seemed only interested in one another's bodies. On New Year's Eve he went alone to a party at the station owner's house, where he drank too much. He thought his behaviour passable until he dropped a crystal punch bowl on the living room floor. Mortification! And again he was in trouble with an owner's wife and thought he might be fired. But the agitation and sleepless nights passed and the shattered punch bowl story became water cooler gossip at the radio station and was then forgotten. As he walked the winter streets of the town or lay reading on his bed in the YMCA room, he wondered how he could get closer to books. Who read the books before they were printed? Who decided their fate? What was looked for? What made one book more appealing than another?

It was the beginning of a new decade, and he was forcing himself to rethink his future, a future he now hoped would be spent among books, either writing them himself or helping others to write them. So how could he find his way into that future with only his jingle writing to recommend him? From the yellow pages of the Toronto telephone book he selected the names of twelve publishing companies and sent each a copy of his letter asking for a chance. He knew it was a long shot, but he was hoping that, out of the twelve, he might find one person who would appreciate his enthusiasm and humour, his love of language. Again his luck held, and though he received only one reply, it was promising. It came from Kildare Dobbs, senior editor at Macmillan of Canada, who said he'd enjoyed reading the letter. It was, he said, funny and different from most applicants' letters; it was also well written, a good start for anyone involved in the publishing business. Dobbs invited him to an interview at 70 Bond Street in downtown Toronto. In his room he read Dobbs's letter over and over. He'd struck gold—an editor with a sense of humour.

Walking the Red Dog

Kildare Dobbs was a heavy-set man in his late thirties then, with a round friendly face, an Anglo-Irish immigrant, a Royal Navy veteran, a Cambridge graduate who had spent time in Africa after the war. He was well read, warm and welcoming, and in the years ahead they would become good friends. Certainly on that April morning in 1960 he knew that he had met a man he wanted to learn from; he can no longer recall the details of that interview, only that it seemed good-natured and hopeful. Dobbs appeared genuinely interested in the young man's ambition to work with words. He had also shown the letter to John Morgan Gray, the president, who also wanted to speak to him, and later that morning they were introduced. The president, a trim compact man in his fifties in a dark suit and tie, with a handkerchief tucked into a coat sleeve, was, in many ways, a formidable presence. Again the young man put forth his case for being close to books while Gray listened, thoughtfully smoking his pipe and smiling and sometimes nodding as if he could remember his own days as a young and eager reader of Hemingway and Sherwood Anderson. But they also talked about hockey. Gray told him he'd played hockey in Europe back in the 1920s. He recounted those days with another smile and had a fund of stories about watching games at Maple Leaf Gardens when Busher Jackson and Charlie Conacher and King Clancy were playing. They had both, it seemed, relaxed into a shared passion. That spring Montreal and Toronto were competing in the Stanley Cup final, and he confessed that he had been a fan of the Montreal Canadiens since the days of childhood shinny games, when he imagined himself always as Maurice "Rocket" Richard. Hearing all this, Gray put down his pipe and said, "Well, I don't suppose I can hold that against you." Leaving the office, the young man couldn't help wondering, Did that mean that everything else then was acceptable? Dobbs said he would give him a call in a few days.

In spite of the cooling off between him and Maxine, he was staying for the weekend at the apartment over the public baths. Getting in touch at the YMCA or at the radio station in Orillia wasn't easy. And so began a weekend of anxious waiting until, on Monday, Dobbs called to say that they would like to try him for three months as a junior editor. They couldn't offer a very princely salary, only sixty dollars a week. He accepted the offer.

The phone call left him so exhilarated (relieved to get the job) but anxious (would he measure up to their expectations?) that he had to walk off his excitement. This would become a lifetime habit whenever he felt the onset of anxiety. His rapid pace was a way of calming himself, and he would always refer to it as "walking the red dog." If, as he had read, depression was called by no less a personage than Winston Churchill the "black dog," then, as far as he was concerned, that dog had a younger brother who could nearly be as troublesome. To restore his emotional equilibrium on that April Monday in 1960, he set out along Queen Street, walking west as far as Roncesvalles Avenue, where he stopped for lunch, and sat thinking of Dobbs's phone call, remembering his use of the word *princely*. The young man had never heard anyone use such a word in conversation. What a hick he really was! But at least he realized it and knew that he now wanted to be in the company of a man who could so casually insert such a word into conversation. Perhaps his future was in publishing. It seemed like an attractive way of life. Somewhere he had read that it was often referred to as an "occupation for gentlemen." And wasn't John Morgan Gray the very epitome of a gentleman? With his pipe and courtly manners, the handkerchief tucked up his sleeve, the ease with which he discussed subjects as diverse as literature and hockey? Back at the apartment, he had finally tired out the red dog and sat thinking that he would do his damndest to succeed at Macmillan. No more commercials for the canned soup specials at the A&P. Now he would put words to better use. He began to think too that when he finally settled into a new place and had perhaps a little money to spare, he would buy a pipe and some Dutch tobacco.

St. Martin's House, now a permanent heritage building, was located at 70 Bond Street, two blocks east of Yonge, a handsome brick building with an elegant brass plate bearing the company's name, Macmillan of Canada. On the main floor a middle-aged receptionist named Robbie sat at a plug-in switchboard greeting callers with a cockney accent that at first to him was a declaration of the company's prosperity, "Good morning, Macmillions of Canada." It would take him a few days to get used to Robbie's accent. He was assigned to a small desk on the third floor, in the Trade Department's editorial offices, the word *trade* denoting books sold by bookstores: novels, histories, biographies, cookbooks, children's books; anything that was not a textbook. Those came from the fourth floor in the Educational Department.

He shared an open space with the president's secretary and another clerical worker; an adjoining sample room displayed the most recently published titles. On this floor were also the offices of Dobbs and Gray. Among his first duties was recording the arrival and almost invariably the hasty departure of manuscripts from what was eponymously referred to as the "slush pile." These were unsolicited manuscripts and arrived inside large brown envelopes or ominously heavy shirt boxes containing the end results of aspiring novelists and poets, soothsayers and astrologers, religious fanatics, philosophically minded crackpots and self-help zealots with their versions of Dale Carnegie's best-seller, *How to Win Friends and Influence People*.

He recorded the title, author's name and date of submission in a huge ledger, which he was soon referring to as the *Book of Doom*, a title he shared with Dobbs, who laughed but warned him not to be sarcastic in the reports he was asked to write. Apparently the boss didn't like it. The report was a one-page summary of the manuscript's content and the reader's assessment of the work. Dobbs also told him that if he saw even a glimmer of hope in the writing, he should recommend another opinion at the Friday morning editorial meeting in Gray's office.

Many of the manuscripts, coffee stained and badly wrinkled, had obviously been glanced at by others. So many people were eager to write yet, even to his relatively untrained eye, ill equipped to do so. At first he carefully read from start to finish, wondering how anyone could write so badly yet remain convinced to the end that what he had was good enough to submit to a publisher. When he asked Dobbs about this, the editor merely smiled. " 'Of making many books there is no end, and much study is a weariness of the flesh.' Those words were written, Dick, about three thousand years ago by some jaded Egyptian. In other words, there will always be people who want to tell their stories, however badly." Sometimes submissions were accompanied by shameless entreaties. "I think you should know that I wrote this book during the week that Mother lay dying." According to Dobbs, encouraging such people meant only trouble. "First thing you know, they turn up at the door, and you can't get rid of them. Meantime they break down in tears and you have a scene on your hands." He paused. "I fear some may have day passes from 999 Queen. Are you familiar with that reference?" He was, having passed the Mental Health Centre by streetcar many times when he was living in the west end of the city, during his first year at Ryerson.

Reading from the slush pile, however, could also provide a bracing dose of *schadenfreude*. He realized that he wasn't raising the bar very high in thinking that he could write better than 95 percent of the submissions he was reading. In an age before "creative writing programs" became popular, he was getting some excellent training in learning how *not* to write a novel. Or anything else for that matter. Of the hundreds of manuscripts he would read over the next three years, he passed on perhaps a dozen to the editor, and he can't remember any of them being published. Small wonder that few publishers, if any, now accept unsolicited work; it's left to literary agents to vet what might or might not be publishable, and they understandably charge for the service. In time he was assigned to writing flap copy for new books, a couple of hundred words to describe and extol the author's work.

In those early days at Macmillan he quickly realized how little he knew about literature and one day on a whim asked Dobbs for a list of books that an educated person interested in literature should read. Dobbs, always a good-natured mentor, recommended some thirty books, of which his pupil had read only half a dozen. Among the titles were Nashe's *The Unfortunate Traveller* and novels by Tobias Smollett and Henry Fielding. There was Dickens's *Hard Times* and Laurence Sterne's *Tristram Shandy*, Frazer's *The Golden Bough*. He read them all and many others with enthusiasm. He would be forever grateful for Dobbs's help and friendship, and sorry when, in 1962, Kildare decided to leave publishing for a life in journalism and freelance writing. They would, however, keep in touch from time to time, mostly in later years at Friday luncheons that attracted journalists and academics, novelists and booksellers and librarians, all under the aegis of the congenial Jack McLeod.

In the early sixties, he also became friends with a new arrival at Macmillan, an Irish immigrant who limped from a sporting accident in youth, Leo Simpson, a craggy-faced Limerick man who joined the Advertising and Publicity Department. In time he too would become a novelist. Leo was also an avid reader, and they would soon spend time after work in the Silver Rail at the corner of Yonge and Shuter, going over the week's work, sharing enthusiasms for writers like Donald Barthelme and Kurt Vonnegut, quoting favourite passages from J. P. Donleavy's *The Ginger Man*, the saucy account of an Irish-American scoundrel drinking and fornicating his way through post-war Dublin. A literary role model for both of them, at least in their imaginations. By then he was living in a Huron Street rooming house.

In the early sixties, the area known as the Annex was affordable for young people, university students or those like himself who were starting careers. A commodious brick house, 496 Huron Street held several tenants who shared bathrooms and kitchens. For a brief but glorious time he was the only male in the house, surrounded by young women. He couldn't believe his luck. By then he had bought his pipe and sometimes in the evenings tucked a foulard around his throat. In blazer and slacks he thought he cut a suave figure, and one young woman said the smell of his pipe in the hallway was "dreamy." He promised to blow a few mouthfuls through her keyhole that night. So there he was, Sebastian Dangerfield at home in Dreamland.

In the autumn of 1962 Khrushchev and Kennedy began playing their deadly chess match with everything at stake, the so-called Cuban missile crisis. It was time to take a holiday. But where could you escape from possible annihilation? The answer wasn't simple, but in a fatalistic mood he decided to go to Europe. He might as well see things he'd always wanted to see, and in October he left for a madcap fifteen-day tour of nine countries beginning in Ireland, where some of his forebears had once lived. In Dublin he paid his respects to one of his literary heroes, Jonathan Swift, in St. Patrick's Cathedral, where the great wit and satirist had once been dean, reading the words inscribed in the white stone of his tomb, the epitaph written by Swift himself. *Ubi saeva indignatio ulterius cor lacerare nequit* (Where savage indignation can lacerate him no longer).

He can remember wondering what Swift would have made of the crisis that was unfolding that October, with the two largest nuclear-armed nations of the world playing a game of "who blinks first." At stake the future of the planet. Was this not historically the most egregious display of our species's hubristic idiocy? To distract himself from such dire ruminations, he walked the streets of Dublin in the footsteps of Stephen Dedalus, enjoying the smoky pubs, striking up conversations with the voluble Irish. But talk everywhere was about Cuba and the standoff between the Yanks and the Russkis. The next day he was in London at the Macmillan offices, near Covent Garden. John Gray had written to the London office about the young Canadian visitor who was eager to see the parent company. Despite the headlines and newscasts, it was business as usual inside the publishing house, where he was invited to sit in on an editorial meeting. Later he lunched with one of the editors, and talking shop was a welcome relief. Two days later he was boarding a ferry at Newhaven for Dieppe, and that afternoon, as the French coast came into sight, he stood by the ship's railing trying to imagine the fear and excitement of the Canadian soldiers only twenty years before as they awaited their first taste of combat on a mission that was doomed to failure. By evening he was in Paris, looking nervously along with others at the headlines in the newspaper stalls along the Seine. Surely it was time for someone, either Russian or American, to come to his senses.

Three days later he was in Vienna, where he went to the Pratergruen, with its merry-go-rounds and beer gardens, and there he took a ride on the huge Ferris wheel, remembering a scene from the 1949 movie *The Third Man*, with Orson Welles as the black market crook Harry Lime explaining the *realpolitik* of life in post-war Vienna to Holly Martins, a pulp novelist, played by Joseph Cotten. As they both look down from the Ferris wheel's carriage, Lime points to tiny human dots below and asks, "Would you really feel any pity if one of those dots stopped moving forever? If I offered you twenty thousand pounds for every dot that stopped, would you really, old man, tell me to keep my money, or would you calculate how many dots you could afford to spare?" In the carriage of that Ferris wheel on a chilly October afternoon in 1962, he remembered sitting with his father in the Capitol Theatre in Midland listening to Orson Welles say the words that were written by Graham Greene.

Two days later on the Ostend train he watched a group of young Germans board at Linz. They were a little drunk, high-spirited and noisy. After looking at their tickets, the conductor left the carriage and the young men began to drink more beer. Soon they were singing Horst Wessel songs and he imagined himself back in the 1930s, in the days of the Hitler Youth movement. All that extravagant enthusiasm of the young in full voice with a hint of threat in the air. Passengers were getting up and moving to the next car. He followed along, and a few minutes later a woman sat down beside him. It was the last seat available, and they both smiled as if agreeing that, while travelling, now and then one has to put up with loutishness. She was in her late thirties or early forties. Her English was quite good. She told him she had never met a Canadian before. She had been visiting an aunt in Vienna and was now on her way home to Brussels.

Her husband was a high-school teacher. She talked about "this Cuban business," as she called it. She had become restless in her compartment and so had come out to talk to someone. Did he mind? No he didn't. What did he think would happen between the Americans and the Russians? He tried to soothe her fears, but he was not good at it, and after a while she took his hand and held it while they looked out the window at the fields and villages passing by. After a time she said quietly, "Would you like to come back to my compartment?"

They made their way along the corridors of the swaying train. Her compartment was big enough for four people, but she told him she had it to herself. After drawing down the blinds on the window, she touched his face and kissed him. He can remember looking through the shuttered blinds at a row of polled plane trees, the avenue to some enormous estate.

The next day in London, he spent the afternoon in a pub on the Strand in the company of a former RAF pilot who had flown Spitfires in the war. The man had pictures of himself standing by an aircraft in his flying suit and grinning at the camera. They talked about the Cuban crisis. "Don't worry," he said, "that fat peasant Khrushchev will back down. He doesn't want to take on the Yanks. He knows they can turn Russia into a graveyard in a matter of minutes." They drank the afternoon away, and he was mildly heartened by the former pilot's optimism. By the time he got back to Canada the next day, the Cuban missile crisis had been resolved, and people could return to their lives.

*

At 70 Bond Street in Toronto, Kildare Dobbs had been replaced by James Bacque, who came from the magazine world.

By then, however, at John Gray's urging, he had moved from the Editorial Department into sales. Gray told him that he had a promising future in publishing, but it was imperative that he gain experience in various aspects of the business, and that included working in both the trade and educational fields. Over the next few years he would travel across the country acquainting himself with booksellers and librarians. His brief stint in the Educational Department confirmed his suspicion that his future would not include "pitching" ideas for textbooks to department heads in schools and colleges. But at least the experience furnished him with a plausible occupation for the narrator of his first novel, *The Weekend Man*.

In 1964 he wrote an adventure story for children eight to ten years old as part of a new series called Buckskin Books. The series had been initiated the previous year and, thanks to a contest, had got off to a good start. But by the second year it was in danger of faltering because of the lack of new titles. Where were the Canadian authors of children's books? At an editorial meeting Gray urged everyone to ask librarians, schoolteachers, *anyone* who might want to try their hand at writing a book for children. When he went home that night, he thought about it and began to wonder if he might not write one himself. He had no particular idea for a story, but it might be fun to try. To avoid putting pressure on colleagues, he decided to submit the manuscript under a pseudonym. By then he had moved to a one-bedroom apartment on Rose Avenue near Bloor and Sherbourne Streets. It took him six weeks of evenings standing at the kitchen counter to write the little book in longhand. Later it would be typed by an intelligent and attractive young woman named Phyllis Cotton, who had recently joined the Trade Department from a clerical position on the second floor. Of course she was sworn to secrecy. In a couple of years she would become his wife.

Andrew Tolliver was a first-person account of a ten-year-old boy who foils a bank robber disguised as John A. Macdonald during a town's centenary of Macdonald's historic visit. A few weeks after he submitted the manuscript he began to hear rumours around the office that the Editorial Department was excited about the prospects of a new juvenile title by someone called Frank Sullivan. At the editorial meeting, John Gray praised the book, but did anyone know who this Frank Sullivan was? As a writer he would come to cherish irony, but this was truly a golden moment as he sat there listening to others praise the little book. After the meeting he approached Gray and asked if he could speak to him privately in his office. He was worried that the president might not be amused by his caper, for he believed that, by and large, most people don't like to be fooled. But Gray was delighted by the news. He told him that as a young man he too had published a book for boys, though he hadn't used another name. But he understood the motive behind the submission. Actually, when the book was published the following year, the manner of its submission provided an interesting introduction to a positive review by Robert Fulford in the *Toronto Star*. *Andrew Tolliver* sold well and, after it went out of print a few years later, was resurrected by a small American publisher under the title *One John A. Too Many,* enjoying a second life in schools throughout Canada and the United States. He would soon discover that one of the delights of writing for children was the eagerness with which they wrote letters, and he always looked forward to receiving those lumpy packages from classrooms of grade fours or fives eager to ask the author questions about the characters. The book's publication was a small but satisfying beginning, and it may have triggered the restlessness that was beginning to emerge in his life.

Without a doubt, publishing had its attractions: the faintly glamorous atmosphere surrounding the lunches and parties, the book launches with their sixties' cigarette smoke and guests sipping martinis; it seemed to him like a beguiling celebration of accomplishment and, accompanying it, a sense of engagement in something worthwhile, namely, the birth of a book. There were conferences for librarians and booksellers where he met intelligent and interesting people. Publishing would never make him rich, but he had never harboured that ambition anyway. It did, however, offer a comfortable living and a great deal of fun and satisfaction.

Yet lurking within all this well-ordered and appealing life was a restiveness that could not be ignored. Every time he read a new novel he wondered if he could match the author's talent. With a particularly good book, he would study the sentence arrangement: the way the author convinced the reader that the characters and story were somehow more real than people he might encounter in ordinary life. He was reading contemporary American fiction eagerly and enviously. Saul Bellow, Philip Roth, Bernard Malamud, Kurt Vonnegut, Thomas Berger. One novel in particular captured him with its uncanny depiction of a man very like himself. This was Louisiana writer Walker Percy's *The Moviegoer*, winner of the 1962 National Book Award, arguably America's most prestigious fiction prize. *The Moviegoer* is narrated by Binx Bolling, a young man who is unsure about where his life is going; he can't seem to fit in anywhere and so concentrates on a kind of inner life. In his search for meaning in a world of terrible uncertainties, Bolling seemed a figure lost in a Cold War world. He read the book three times, seeing in the narrator's plight a mirror image of his own life. Not since he'd read Camus's *The Outsider* had a novel so enthralled him, almost urging him on toward a new direction. Could he write a book that so vividly and amusingly portrayed confusion? Had he not been thinking about writing most of his life? In the past few years, he had surrounded himself with books and kept company with people who worked with books. But how could he now find the time to write a book himself? His job often required travel. To Vancouver or Montreal or New York. How could he carve a couple of hours a day out of that kind of life? Was he prepared to give up his job with its decent salary. He wasn't sure he was quite ready to take the plunge.

Yet he often felt lonely and dissatisfied with his life. The birth control pill had taken the worry out of being close, and there was no shortage of sex in the 1960s. It was all out there, so help yourself. In fact, have a second helping. But the entanglements; the painful closing down of relationships that were going no-where, ending often in tearful profanity and then followed by more of the same on the telephone at three o'clock in the morn-ing. He began to realize that the only woman he was really in-terested in was Phyllis Cotton, and he began to spend more time with her. He was fascinated by her background, a Gaspé girl from a large family, her father a fisherman who saw his liveli-hood ending with draggers cleaning out the last of the fish. He would eventually move his family to Toronto. By then Phyllis had already left for Montreal to stay with relatives and work. She told him of those early days in Montreal, of walking by the McGill campus on lunch hours and looking at the students on their way to classrooms, wondering if she would ever have the opportunity to be a part of all that. In fact, in time she would enter that very world, earning three degrees and pursuing a successful career as an academic librarian. But in the mid-sixties she was just a young woman, endlessly curious about how the world worked. They talked often about what was worth doing in life. In time they became lovers, and they were married in the summer of 1966 in Toronto at the Church of St. Simon-the-Apostle. The following year their first son, Christopher, was born, and they moved from the tiny apartment on Rose Avenue to a rented bungalow on Elm Road near Lawrence Avenue. He was thirty years old that year, a young businessman getting on the Avenue Road southbound bus each morning with other businessmen, mildly bemused by the turmoil of the times.

The war in Vietnam had dramatically changed the dynamics of literary and cultural life in the country, particularly in cities like Toronto and Montreal and Vancouver. An influx of young Americans, some avoiding the military draft, was attracted to teaching jobs in new universities opening across the country. Streets like Yorkville and Hazelton in the centre of Toronto were swarming on weekend nights with disaffected teenagers from the suburbs. A spirit of nationalism, perhaps rooted in anti-Americanism, led to the emergence of small publishing houses, like Coach House Press and House of Anansi, devoted exclusively to promoting Canadian literature. The hippie movement was under way as young people, disillusioned with big business and America's hawkish foreign policies, left urban life behind and settled in the countryside, in communes.

His friend Leo Simpson was no hippie, but he and his wife, Jackie, shared the dream of many by moving to a farm in Eastern Ontario, where Jackie secured a teaching job at a local high school. He envied Leo's determination and commitment to write, and he and Phyllis often visited the Simpsons on weekends to drink and talk about books and writing. He can remember one Sunday morning in particular when Leo and Jackie and Phyllis went for a walk. He begged off! Was that intended? Perhaps because after they left he climbed the stairs to Leo's writing room. Ever the snoop, he was anxious to see how his friend was getting on with his book. But perhaps it was something else. Perhaps he just wanted to see the room where it was all taking place. And so he can remember entering the sunlit space and examining Leo's desk, with its dictionary and thesaurus, the pencil shavings and the shreds of rubber from the eraser that had rubbed out a word or perhaps a sentence. The small cup holding pens and pencils. The desk of a working writer in those days. How he admired his friend's devotion to his craft, his days spent alone with words.

Yet for him it seemed an impossible dream. Now they had a child, and the chances of his wife finding work in the immediate future were slim. He had been in publishing long enough to know that most writers lived from book to book or had teaching jobs or private incomes. Nearly all seemed to be on the edge of hard times. But the urge was there and often seemed irresistible; moreover, he was pleased by his wife's conviction that he should give his dream of writing a chance to succeed. And she had an idea on how to make it work. Since money was a major obstacle, perhaps there was a way around it. Obviously it would be too expensive to stay in Toronto, but what if they moved for a year to her family house on the Gaspé coast? Since the family had moved to Toronto, the house in Barachois was now used only for summer holidays. It was there empty and waiting for free. They talked about this night after night, lying in bed, making plans, abandoning them for others, reviewing their circumstances, their chances for success or failure. It was exciting, as possibilities for a change in life always are. But could he deal with the uncertainties that would accompany a year of living off their savings with no income? Just thinking about it sometimes awakened the red dog, who had to be taken out at once for a brisk walk along the dark streets of the city after midnight. Finally one evening, Phyllis, doubtless impatient with his dithering, said, "Let's not just talk about this, we've talked it out. Let's get on with it." And so they did.

A House by the Sea

When Phyllis told her parents of their plans, they were understandably surprised and puzzled. They could hardly have been expected to be pleased, and he tried to imagine how it must have looked to his father-in-law, a man he both liked and admired. Why would a young man with a wife and child to support leave a good steady job in Toronto to live for a year in Gaspé writing a book? It must have seemed incomprehensible to him, though he was too polite to say so. He asked his daughter if her husband realized that he would have to split five cords of wood to see them through the winter. Had he ever split wood in his life? No doubt her father was worried about his daughter and grandson enduring months of cold and snow with a man who didn't seem like a prime candidate for survival. And who could blame him for feeling that way? He came from a tradition in which people didn't take chances if they didn't have to. Yet in April, almost eight years to the day from his hiring, he told

John Gray he was leaving, going to the Gaspé to try to write a novel. Gray was disappointed but sympathetic, confessing that at one point early in his publishing life he too had thought of becoming a writer.

Phyllis's parents still returned to the Gaspé for two weeks each summer, and that July in 1968 she and their one-year-old son, Christopher, accompanied them while he stayed behind to settle matters with the bank and the insurance agent. A week later at five o'clock in the morning he too set forth in their five-year-old Volkswagen, packed with books and old vinyl LPs. As it turned out they would not be able to play those recordings until September, when their furniture finally arrived.

Starting a new life brings with it the promise of hope and the adventures of change, but with it too the fears of failure. But driving eastward through Quebec that summer with the windows down, he felt that this was a good move, an opportunity at last to do something that had been foremost in his mind since he had finished the children's book. And so he was happy enough, he supposed, as he passed by or went through the towns of eastern Quebec: Rivière-du-Loup, Trois-Pistoles, Rimouski, Matane, Cap-Chat, Sainte-Anne-des-Monts. Then farther eastward to the very edge of the whale-shaped Gaspé Peninsula and the village of Barachois.

From the beginning the rugged landscape and sea intrigued him. He loved the coastal weather with its dramatic changes; a cloudless morning with a blazing sunrise could change to sheets of rain by noon, but within a few hours the sky would clear to a gorgeous sunset and a star-filled night. He was reading Rachel Carson's *The Sea Around Us* and Henry Beston's *The Outermost House*. Published in 1928, the book described a year on the Great Beach of Cape Cod, almost a thousand miles south of them. Perhaps in imitation of Beston's book, he began a journal, his first entries predictably little more than weather reports, which he wrote in longhand at a small desk in an upstairs bedroom that overlooked the Gulf of St. Lawrence.

Sunday, August 4/68
Morning rain with heavy clouds. Muggy. Clearing by noon with light winds. NW 68F.
Another fine sunset and spectacular moonrise over the sea.

He liked to think of these entries as warm-up exercises while he waited for a story to emerge. He had arrived without a clear idea of what to write. Or was that really true? He seems to recall having an inkling of a story, but perhaps not. In any case he now sat each morning at the little desk looking out at the sea and scribbling notes.

That summer they bought five cords of wood, and he borrowed an axe from Phyllis's uncle Isaac, who was still fishing. Isaac Lemieux and his wife, Vida, would be invaluable in helping them get through that year and would become lifelong friends. After lunch each day he went to work with the axe and in time got used to the rhythm involved in splitting firewood. He actually enjoyed the work, especially toward the end of the afternoon, when he stacked the wood in the basement in six neat rows. At the same time, the physical work enabled him to think about the book he wanted to write and it also kept the red dog away. Already he could imagine a young man, a publisher's salesman living somewhere in the suburbs of Toronto, a man not unlike himself though separated from an ambitious wife and handicapped son, a man bewildered by the modern world with its incessant consumerism and constant need for distraction while everything and everyone lay under the shadow of nuclear annihilation. How was one to live in such a world?

In time he would capture the comic despair in the voice of Wes Wakeham, the narrator of his first novel, *The Weekend Man*. After writing the opening pages he knew that it would be a comic novel, its tone immediately appropriated by his natural inclination to be satirical. After it was published he would be happily astonished at how the book resonated with so many readers who wrote to him about enjoying, among other things, one of Wakeham's quirky strategies for combating existential boredom.

This morning the sunlight dances off the snow and makes the eyes water. Below my window the whine of spinning tires burns the air as some unfortunate worker begins his Thursday in a snowbank, up to his frozen ballocks in the white stuff and already late for the meetings and decisions.

I breakfast on Rice Krispies, whole-wheat toast and Instant Sanka, the luck of the draw. On the counter of my kitchenette are two glass jars formerly holding Peter Pan Peanut Butter. Now each contains several slips of paper. One jar is lettered "Breakfast Menus" and the other, "Routes to the Office." Each weekday morning I close my eyes and draw forth one piece of paper from each jar. I have about a dozen breakfast menus in the one: simple meals like Special "K" with cracked-wheat toast and cocoa, boiled egg, English muffin and tea, Banana Instant Breakfast—things like that. If I didn't leave my choice to the impersonal decisions of Chance, I know I would end up doing what my father did every working day of his life: sitting down before a bowl of cornflakes and two pieces of white toast. And I know that sooner or later this would sneak up and get me in strange ways.

The same with going to work. I have laid out eighteen routes to the office—some of them quite tricky, involving dead-end crescents and one-way streets. It can take me anything from five minutes to half an hour to get to work in the morning, depending on which piece of paper I draw from the peanut-butter jar. The shortest and most direct way, of course, is along Union Avenue to Britannia Road and north for a few blocks—the route I travel homeward each evening. The half-hour trip which I have called the Jumbo Route is a knotty criss-cross affair in which I avoid all the big avenues and take to the back streets of Union Place, always watching carefully for the little children who sometimes disobey Elmer the Safety Elephant and dart out from behind parked cars. I've only drawn the Jumbo once since I started working at Winchester House.

Working on it that year, he wondered from time to time if it was all just an act of revenge for all those afternoons spent waiting in schools in Scarborough or Markham for department heads to appear and listen or not as he addressed the virtues of his wares, and then left, crossing the parking lot to his car with a satchel of spellers and readers.

The furniture they had arranged to send by transport in June had not yet arrived by September. With no telephone in the house, they relied on a phone booth in front of the general store, and there he asked for an explanation for the delay. Three months can be a long time without a refrigerator, he said to the woman in Toronto. The unhelpful answer was that, since they had moved to such a remote area, it wasn't worthwhile to send a half-empty van. The transport company was waiting for other people who might wish to move to Gaspé in the near future. It seemed to him a strange way to run a trucking company and he told her so, wryly pointing out that it was like being sold a bus ticket and then turning up the next day for the journey, only to be informed that the bus only travels there when it's full. The woman wasn't into humour and hung up on him. In desperation he turned to the *Toronto Star*, remembering a consumer column that was supposed to help people who felt they were being shafted by big business. He poured out his tale of woe without much hope, but, to his surprise, it worked. The transport company it seemed had been publicly shamed into service, and his family's worldly goods arrived a week later.

He had almost forgotten the convenience and pleasure of a few appliances: food storage and music now from the big spinning vinyl discs on their Clairtone stereo, Mozart and Schubert, old friends in out of the cold. On an autumn evening of wind and rain with a glass of whisky, and Turgenev's *A Sportsman's Notebook* in hand, the Trout Quartet playing, his wife reading in another chair by the kitchen stove, his one-year-old son staggering around the kitchen in the first stages of self-locomotion, it was easy to imagine that he had made the right choice. At such times he liked to step outside and stand in the rainy darkness for just a few moments, listening to the sea on the far edge of the sandbar, with the surf thudding onto the shore. Then return to the warm kitchen, to his wife and son and dinner. Upstairs in his workroom, a growing pile of manuscript pages covered with his words. Now made into sentences and paragraphs and chapters. Shelter and warmth and food. The elemental nature of it all appealed to him. It wouldn't always be this idyllic, but while it was, it was worth noting, savouring and above all remembering with words.

Sometimes anxiety overtook him, leaving him sleepless and fearful. He had moved his family to this remote corner of the country to indulge himself. They were living off their savings, which with careful management would last a year or so. But he had no experience at earning money in other writerly ways: reviewing books or writing articles; journalism wasn't his métier. At such times he imagined the presence of old Puritan forebears whispering admonitions about the frivolousness of writing a storybook. By Christmas the winter had delivered its winds and snow, and it would continue for another four months. But in many ways it was everything he thought it might be. A good place to write and a good place to enjoy family life in an uncomplicated way. The day before Christmas he carried his son through the snow to the top of the hill behind the house, where he cut down a spruce tree for the season. It was a sunlit morning of pure cold beauty. Remember this, he said to himself. Try to remember this happiness.

January brought storm after storm. They were virtually buried in snow, and when the plow went by a wall of snow obscured the highway. He cut steps in the snowbank down to the road. They brought their groceries home on the child's sleigh. But so what? They weren't going anywhere. Sometimes he worried about an emergency. The hospital in Gaspé was fifty kilometres away, but he imagined they would cope. Other people along the coast did. On weekend afternoons they skated on the bay and he coached a local hockey team. They attended parties with rela-

Barachois, Gaspé—House in
winter—A February day in 1969.

tives and neighbours. Everything seemed to slow down, and he
lived in the moment. By the following summer they had guests
who were curious about their retreat from the rest of the world.
He had set himself a deadline of October to finish his book, and
he made it with two weeks to spare. After his wife finished typ-
ing the last draft, they prepared to leave. His plan was to find
work in publishing again, perhaps for a year, and then enroll at
a university in the hope of eventually becoming a teacher. That
seemed the best way to finance a life of writing. With this in
mind he had sent letters to several publishers and was surprised
to receive a half-dozen replies expressing interest.

That last week he felt good about everything. He thought

his book was publishable, though you could never be sure. Still he was eager to re-enter the other world, have the book read. Get on with things. Yet the night before they left he lay rigid in bed unable to sleep, getting up a half-dozen times to step out on the veranda for a leak, always a sign of anxiety. Staring up at the star-filled autumn sky. The beauty of all that emptiness. What used to be called the heavens. Then back into the house and a quick look into his two-year-old son's crib. At what age did the threat of crib death subside? But the child was sleeping deeply and peacefully. He told himself to settle down while he quietly opened cupboard doors and—For goodness' sake, what was this? Why, a bottle with two or three inches of whisky still in it. No point in leaving that, and it would definitely be unwise to travel with an opened bottle of whisky in the car. Suppose they had an accident? He saw himself being questioned by a cop about the whisky bottle. No, no, this had to be emptied, and not down the sink either.

Sitting in the rocking chair in the quiet dark house he sipped whisky and water, felt the symptoms of anxiety receding: the cold hands and feet, the shivering, the need to urinate. It was all slipping away while his wife and son slept. He hadn't made a penny in over a year and funds were getting low. But they were young and healthy and surely one of the half-dozen publishers would hire him. They would find a place to live and they would send out the manuscript and get on with life. So he told himself to drink up, enjoy the moment. Get a little shut-eye before their journey. One last piss and a final gander at a sky so clear of pollution that it probably looked the same as it did a thousand years ago. So he had taken a year off the write a novel? He wouldn't be the first or the last to do that, and perhaps a publisher would be sympathetic. "I understand the impulse, Richard. I've felt like it myself at times before I settled into work. You'll be just fine. You've got that out of your system. Welcome to the firm." In the rocking chair he finished the whisky. It was three o'clock in the morning and he was mildly drunk. Three o'clock in the morning! Didn't someone write a song about that? Wasn't it mentioned in *The Great Gatsby*? Oh, the advantages of a literary education.

A few hours later he was awake and the red dog was barking in his ear. He felt he was coming apart at the seams like an old suit worn once too often. All this on a lovely morning in October. He didn't say much, moving carefully about the house packing things into the car. But his wife had now lived with him long enough to recognize the onset of these attacks and counselled deep breathing. She said she'd drive, and so he sat with a racing heart in the back seat of the little car with his son. The deep breathing helped, but it wasn't enough to stop him from wanting to urinate every ten minutes or quell his racing heartbeat. Two hours later they stopped at the hospital in Murdochville, a copper-mining town in the mountains. In the emergency ward a young doctor plunged a needle into his hip. It was the first time he experienced diazepam, but it wouldn't be the last. Within a few minutes he felt himself relaxing, the agitation settling and then disappearing. The young doctor (may he live to be a hundred and ten in some sunny haven!) wrote a prescription for twenty tablets known under the trade name of Valium; in those days it was the drug of choice for anxiety sufferers, though in the next decade, through overuse by harried housewives and starlets, it came to be over-prescribed and caused problems. But in that fall of 1969, the little pills steadied him while they stayed briefly at his wife's parents' in Toronto. It was crowded because Phyllis had five siblings. He was sure her family felt that she and her husband had wasted a year of life, though no one said anything about it.

Within a couple of weeks, however, they found an apartment in Don Mills and he was hired as a salesman by Oxford University Press with its offices nearby. After lunch with an affable Englishman, Roger Boulton, and the president, Ivon Owen, he accepted a position that was supposed to lead to Vancouver as OUP's permanent rep in British Columbia. He needed the money, and so there was a good deal of underhanded head nodding since he actually hoped to be enrolled at university by September. While listening to this conversation about his future at OUP, he kept thinking absurdly of a favourite childhood film, *Pinocchio,* and the little wooden boy's nose growing with each falsehood. He still fancies the notion that at the lunch from time to time he was touching his own nose.

No matter, he was hired and would begin his duties on the first day of the 1970s, a decade of remorseless asininity with its runaway inflation and bad haircuts. But for a while at least, he would be marching right along, in step with others, resembling to a remarkable degree the character he had invented for his first novel with satchel in hand and a look of affable puzzlement for all. Yet a certain insouciance was now evident. At times he felt giddy and when alone might even be seen trying a few steps *à la* Fred Astaire in *Top Hat* because on November 15, 1969, Macmillan had accepted his novel, and the editor, Ramsay Derry, said they would publish the following September. Now he could legitimately call himself a writer, but he did so only to himself, adopting a lighthearted approach to the business world, writing little notes, perhaps to be read in his dotage to remind him how he felt on such and such a day in his early thirties. This entry for example from a January Monday of that new decade,

This morning at 8:17. Walking along Don Mills Road on my way to a sales conference. Stopped before a huge sign identifying the office buildings behind it. Multiple Access Corp. National Motivation Inc. Now those are muscular words. Makes you want to roll your sleeve up right here on the sidewalk. Something out of Kurt Vonnegut, or the futuristic fantasies of Ray Bradbury. Never mind, my step is light, dare I say even jaunty, my smile betokening a willingness to join the Big Parade. In my new attaché case, three sales memos, a tuna fish sandwich and a paperback copy of Zorba the Greek.

Or this,

Wednesday, Jan. 7/70. 4:32 P.M. A colleague, an earnest young fellow, came over to my desk and handed me a copy of the Royal Bank's monthly newsletter. "You'll find some interesting stuff in this," he said. "It's quite useful." "You bet," I said.

In February OUP sent him west to sell their spring list, an unpromising one, he thought, though it included a revised edition of the New English Bible, which Oxford people had great hopes for. In truth, he can no longer remember many details of that trip beyond making a spectacle of himself in the dining room of the Hotel Vancouver while reading Philip Roth's recently published *Portnoy's Complaint*. A man laughing alone in a restaurant can be an unsettling sight, suggesting either drunkenness or dementia. Who knows? Such a creature laughing away might suddenly cross the room with a steak knife aimed at your throat. But Roth's book was so funny that he couldn't help himself nor do much about the middle-aged couple not far off frowning at him. When they passed his table on their way out, the man aired his annoyance in a tony English accent. Something about "how terribly amusing the book must be."

"Yes," he replied with a smile. "It is a very funny book and very dirty, too. You'd love it." The smart alec in him emerging yet again. But perhaps they both deserved it. Later he repaired to the bar and drank late into the night with an amiable screenwriter from Hollywood, of all places, in town to see someone next day at the CBC about a possible film. Or an impossible one.

In bed that night he lay wondering if, by some terrible coincidence, as a retributive levy on smart alecs, for instance, God had arranged for the disapproving couple in the hotel restaurant to be connected to the book trade. Perhaps the man ran an ecclesiastical bookshop. Had there not been a rather sacerdotal air about him? Perhaps he ran the Anglican Book Centre, where the young salesman had hoped to fatten his blank order book the next day with the sale of New English Bibles. Who would order Bibles from a smart alec who enjoyed dirty books? These are the kinds of nonsensical speculations that fuel anxiety in certain people at two o'clock in the morning.

*

In the 1970s Canadian publishing seemed almost like a cottage industry. The precious few who cared about literature could listen to Robert Weaver's *Anthology* on Saturday nights after the hockey game on CBC radio. Or they could subscribe to *The Tamarack Review*. But no spotlight shone on Canadian writing. No Giller Prize with its swanky televised celebration of Canadian authors. Small independent companies like Coach House Press and House of Anansi published poetry and fiction, and there was an enthusiastic nationalism within the ranks of their authors and poets, fuelled, he used to think, more by anti-Americanism than by any particular love of Canada. In any case he considered it a parochial approach to writing fiction or poetry.

When *The Weekend Man* was published, that September, it attracted little attention, apart from three positive reviews, one by Robert Fulford in *Saturday Night,* and one each from Marian Engel in *The Globe and Mail* and Peter Sypnowich in the *Star.* As the weeks passed he began to wonder if, like many novels, *The Weekend Man* would soon be consigned to oblivion on the remainder tables of second-hand bookstores. After all, he had been in publishing long enough to know that it was the fate of the vast majority of novels. Like those of butterflies, their life-span was short, often lasting only as long as the few months of their first publishing season. A dispiriting thought to be sure.

It seemed, however, that his amiably baffled antihero had charmed some people outside the country, and in the late autumn he was heartened by the enthusiasm for the book from one of America's foremost literary publishers, Farrar, Straus & Giroux, who would bring it out the following spring. Word began to circulate, and suddenly there was interest from publishers in England, Sweden, Germany, France and Japan. Warner Bros. was interested in film rights. This was heady stuff, though he knew enough not to get too excited, especially about film rights. By then he was a thirty-three-year-old student at Trent University, attending seminars and lectures with eighteen-year-olds who had no idea they had a live novelist in their midst. He and Phyllis, who was now pregnant with their second child, had rented a winterized cottage on Chemong Lake for seventy-five dollars a month, and they would live there between Labour Day and the end of May for the next four years. They could scarcely have lived more modestly. Their little Volkswagen was showing signs of age, and, with another child on the way, he was anxious to save as much money as he could. For all the surrounding enthusiasm from New York, money arrived sporadically: a translation advance for a few hundred dollars here and there. He applied for and received a Canada Council grant. But the era of public readings and the teaching of creative writing classes had not yet arrived, and so there was constant worry about money. He was, however, on course, determined to write *and* eventually secure a teaching job. That at least was reassuring.

He was also busy now on his second novel, working in the early morning before going to classes. This would become a lifetime habit, and he always began with a nervous look at the previous day's writing. Did that last paragraph work? Was a particular character underdeveloped? Was she in fact needed at all? Something was lacking, but what? A dozen criticisms surfacing to torment him. Flaws that could paralyze him with dejection. At such times he fell back on his father's advice about shovelling a path through the snow to the street: "Just go through and don't try to make it perfect. You can widen it later." Yes, he knew he had to overcome this compulsion to tinker endlessly with his sentences. Fix it later. Nobody writes a perfect sentence on the first attempt. He knew that by now. But he was also ruefully aware of how such foibles were an integral part of his very nature and therefore extremely difficult to suppress. "Just tell your story," he kept repeating like a mantra. This second novel was resisting him, calling more on his imagination in its portrayal of a middle-aged man trying to find his way through a world he doesn't understand. An older version of Wes Wakeham, though he hoped it wasn't quite that obvious. A more complex man in many ways, Freddy Landon was middle-aged, a greeting card writer with an estranged wife. He could now detect glimpses of certain Saul Bellow characters in his work. But then Bellow was not a bad model. Or was he? More doubts.

They had expected their second child to arrive some time in late January and had placed their firstborn son in the care of his aunt in Toronto. But their second boy, Andrew, obstinately refused to arrive in spite of two trips to the hospital in Peterborough near the end of that month. In the first week of February he took a picture of Phyllis, heavily pregnant, wielding a snow shovel in the laneway in an effort to speed up matters. Then on a Friday night a week or so later, she awakened to say that her labour pains had begun. It was time to move and he did. It was past eleven o'clock when he stepped out to start the car. It had been raining earlier in the afternoon, but now it was freezing rain and the car was coated with ice. The door lock was frozen solid, and he wondered if anyone could hear his curses above the falling ice rain. But few were out on such a night. He briefly thought of going to the gas station at the top of the lane, but it was in darkness. Finally, standing by the car, he reared back and high-kicked the door with his winter boot. Somehow the gods were listening and had heard enough of his anguish for one night and he was able to insert the key and open the door. The little car coughed briefly, slowly chugging into a steady idling while he got busy cleaning the windows. The highway was a skating rink, and getting up the laneway would have to be done in one take. Any slippage backwards might land them in the ditch. With his wife safely in the back seat, he gunned the Volkswagen in first gear up the winding laneway and onto Highway 28, blessedly free of any cars. Not even the salting trucks were out yet, and so they made their way slowly and carefully down the twelve kilometres to Peterborough and St. Joseph's Hospital.

He spent the night in the waiting room half in and half out of sleep, and the baby was born at eight o'clock the next morning. That day the freezing rain turned to snow, and it didn't stop for the next three days. But he didn't care. He was happy from the moment he saw that his wife was sleeping with their new son, both of them exhausted. He wanted now to get back to the cottage before the roads became impassable. But first he stopped for a few groceries and a bottle of Duff Gordon, a cheap but reliable brandy, tolerable with a dash of soda water. The Duffy as he called it was a modest replacement for the light scotches, the J & B and the Cutty Sark, that he had favoured in his publishing days. Economically, of course, he was going downhill, but there was nothing to be gained from dwelling on the fact that publishers lived higher off the hog than the people who wrote the books they sold.

In the cottage he had a couple of Duffys and heated a can of beef stew, hoping it wouldn't be too toxic. It was time to count his blessings. Looking out the window at the snow-covered lake, he thought he might as well have been in Siberia. He was only a little drunk, but so what? His wife and sons were safe and so was he. Things in general weren't so bad. He was on a path toward a degree and would be forever grateful to Trent University for letting him in the door despite his disgraceful high-school grades. But then why should a man be harried all his life because he was such a jerk in high school? *The Weekend Man* would have a second life in April, and he had started a new book. And why not another small Duffy to celebrate that? And another to toast his son's coming into the world. He was alone and drunk in a cottage on the edge of a lake looking out at the mother of all fucking snowstorms. How Canadian was that? Was living in Canada a matter of survival as the nationalists insisted? Maybe. If the beef stew didn't do him in, he would be okay. Opening an anthology of poetry, he looked for Yeats's "A Prayer for My Daughter," which the great poet wrote to celebrate his daughter's birth years before in Ireland on another stormy night. And now the poet's words were with him in a cottage in Canada; so he read them aloud to the mice listening overhead in the attic.

> *Once more the storm is howling, and half hid*
> *Under this cradle-hood and coverlid*
> *My child sleeps on.*

That April *The Weekend Man* was published in the USA and England to enthusiastic reviews, including *The New York Times* and *The Times Literary Supplement*. There was interest in translation rights from publishers in ten countries. Farrar, Straus &

Giroux took out a full-page ad in the *Sunday Times Book Review*, and the novel was an alternate choice for the Book-Of-The-Month Club. All this for a novel that had virtually expired in his own country just a few months before. A sobering thought! Later that year he had drinks with producer Ulu Grosbard and writer Norman Klenman in the roof bar of the Park Plaza in Toronto. They talked about a film version of *The Weekend Man*, and, though nothing came of it, the option money over the next few years was useful.

Time-out at Milford Bridge Cottage, Wootton, Oxfordshire, 1973.

In the spring of 1972 he went to England with his family, eager to work on his second novel. Through a friend they rented Milford Bridge Cottage, a small stone house at the foot of a long hill on the edge of the Oxfordshire village of Wootton, eight miles north of the city. He was told that the road next to their cottage might very well have been used by Shakespeare homeward bound on horseback after an overnight stay at a favourite Oxford inn where, it was rumoured, he had a mistress, namely the innkeeper's wife. True or not, it was a good story, and that summer when Kildare Dobbs visited them, they walked together along that road, speculating on the playwright making his way toward Stratford on his rented horse. That road and the village itself would remain forever in his memory, figuring forth in his imagination four decades later as a setting for a novel entitled *Mr. Shakespeare's Bastard*.

One day shortly after their arrival he walked the eight miles into Oxford and for five pounds bought a second-hand bicycle, a sturdy machine with a big wicker basket strapped to the handlebars. It would be their only means of transportation, his wife using it to cycle into Woodstock for supplies she could not find in the village. Soon they were known as "the young Canadian family in Milford Bridge Cottage," and Phyllis became friends with some of the young mothers in Wootton. They enrolled their five-year-old son in the local school. In the evenings in the King's Head, the writer talked to the farm labourers on topics as old as agricultural life itself: the weather, the crops and the squire's parsimony. On Friday evenings they hired a girl to care for the children and they walked to Woodstock, stopping for drinks in pubs along the way. Sometimes arriving home after these evenings, and still restless, he would take out the bicycle and ride along the dark roads, enjoying the exhilaration of speeding down the hills past the big trees and fields, slowing to pull onto the verge when he saw the lights of an approaching car. He always stopped for a nightcap at the village's other pub, the Killingworth Castle, a tonier drinking hole than the King's Head, with a younger crowd and a sprinkling of the local gentry in their tweeds and caps and plus-fours, the very subjects of the labourers' scorn.

A Cultured Madman?

They returned to Canada in early September, the day after eleven Israelis were murdered by Palestinian terrorists. The newspapers were filled with images of massacre. After their idyllic summer in the English countryside, they were suddenly and brutally returned to the in-your-face news coverage of the world's viciousness. He was glad to get back to Chemong Lake to work on his book, which he would finish in a few months. While he was in England he had been graduated with a B.A. in English and history at Trent University's spring convocation. He was now ready to pursue a career in teaching, but like Dunstan Ramsay in Robertson Davies's *Fifth Business*, he would apply only to private schools, which didn't necessarily demand a teaching certificate. Like Ramsay, he too "didn't want to waste another year getting that." He also agreed with Ramsay's pointed assessment of teachers in general.

I like the company of most of my colleagues who were about equally divided among good men who were good teachers, awful men who were awful teachers, and the grotesques and misfits who drift into teaching and are so often the most educative influences a boy meets in school. If a boy can't have a good teacher, give him a psychological cripple or an exotic failure to cope with; don't just give him a bad dull teacher. This is where the private schools score over the state-run schools; they can accommodate a few cultured madmen on the staff without having to offer explanations.

Truer perhaps fifty years ago than today, but in 1973 he hoped at least he might qualify as one of the cultured madmen.

In the late fall he launched another of his letter-writing campaigns for employment, receiving a few "perhaps in the future when we have an opening" replies. Only one school, Lakefield College, offered something concrete, and after an interview with the headmaster, he was invited to teach a creative writing course for senior students for the spring term. A beginning at least, and he accepted the offer.

With advances from publishers in New York, London and Toronto for his second novel, *In the Middle of a Life,* they were solvent again, and as the May 24 weekend deadline to vacate the cottage drew closer, he and Phyllis talked about where they might go for the summer. To Gaspé perhaps? Or what about returning to England? How about Mexico? Or Ireland? he suggested. His wife was game, but why Ireland? He didn't really know. Put it down to whim. He had visited Ireland briefly in 1962 and perhaps wanted to see more of the country his father's ancestors had emigrated from in the early nineteenth century, settling in Mariposa Township, Victoria County, Ontario. His great-great-grandfather William Wright had registered his two hundred acres from the Crown in 1848, though apparently he and his family had lived on the land since 1834 and had probably arrived in Canada in the 1820s, no doubt vomiting their way across the stormy Atlantic in steerage, his great-grandfather, after whom he was named, travelling in his mother's womb. That Richard Wright would be born in Cavan, Ontario, in 1826 and would live into his nineties, expiring finally in March 1917. His father used to tell him stories of "Old Grandpa" sitting in the kitchen of the farmhouse spitting tobacco juice into the fire in the kitchen stove, often missing the flames. It always seemed to him a strange notion that his father had been that close to a man born so long ago.

Very well then, there was this distant kinship with his Irish ancestry, but what else would attract him? He supposed it was the country's literary heritage. He loved Joyce's *Dubliners,* and for a while *A Portrait of the Artist as a Young Man* had been for him the closest thing to a Bible. Joyce's masterpiece *Ulysses* he put aside fifty pages in on more than one occasion, finishing it with admiration only in middle age. For reasons he could not identify, the poetry of W. B. Yeats filled him with a peculiar sense of longing. He was also beginning to appreciate Beckett's bleak humour. In truth, however, he had to admit that at the end of May 1973 he took his family to Ireland on a whim.

Whim: a sudden fancy; idle and passing notion; capricious idea or desire.

Yes, indeed, a sudden fancy, and he may even have said this aloud as he sat at the bar of a hotel on O'Connell Street in Dublin. It was the second night after their arrival, and he imagined that his audible remark had occasioned strange looks from others, but, as he would soon discover, eccentric observations out of the blue were neither unusual nor unwelcome in Dublin bars. The Irish were perfectly at ease with peculiarity in whatever guise. Anyway, he reminded himself on his third or fourth Jameson that he wasn't being entirely irresponsible. His wife and two sons were above him, sleeping in a comfortable room. But not cheap, by Jaysus, as they said in that city. The pound notes would soon disappear if they stayed too long in hotels. On that second day, while his family had toured the city in a bus, he had gone in search of accommodation with a real estate agent, Desmond O'Leary. It had been at best a dispiriting adventure. Never had he seen such squalid surroundings, and most listed at outrageous prices. And yes, he told the bartender, he would have another, and was that really the red dog at the other end of the bar with a Guinness in front of him?

Now look, he said, this time to himself, things really aren't that bad. They had money in the bank and his second novel would be out in the fall. He had also been commissioned by the CBC to write, of all things, a television play. For this he had received a cheque for two thousand dollars. How do you like them apples? As for the play, he had only the title. *Sundays Are for Henry James*. In many respects this was a dubious project since he knew very little about Henry James beyond the impression that the man constructed elephantine sentences in the service of stories that appeared to be seamlessly inert. A great artist no doubt, but not to his taste. Yet he seemed incapable of ridding himself of this chimeric play's title. It adhered to his imagination like Krazy Glue. Still, he didn't have to return the money to the corporation, and he had the summer ahead of him to work on the bloody thing. His main concern at the moment was where to house his family.

His day with the Realtor's salesman had been fraught with doubts and suspicions. They had met that morning at nine o'clock in front of the hotel just as he was saying goodbye to his wife and sons, who were off on their sightseeing tour. O'Leary was a large expansive man in his fifties or so with red cheeks and a drinker's nose, which put the writer in mind of the hapless Bardolph in the first part of *Henry IV* suffering under Falstaff's merciless teasing.

> *Thou art admiral, thou bearest the lanthorn*
> *in the poop, but 'tis in the nose of thee: thou*
> *art the Knight of the Burning Lamp.*

After his family left on a big green double-decker, O'Leary said, "A fine looking family, Mr. Wright, if I may say so," adding as they walked toward a small Ford estate wagon, "And what may I ask brings you to Dublin?" He probably shouldn't have, but he told O'Leary that he was a writer who had come to Ireland for a change of scenery. O'Leary was enthusiastic at the news. "A writer, you say. Well, well." And there followed inevitable questions about what he wrote and were his books available in Dublin? But he quickly sensed that each regarded the other as a fraud. There was a suspicious grandiosity in O'Leary, while he himself probably looked too young to be a writer of any note. But never mind, they were soon on their way in the estate wagon and looking at flats in the centre of town. Now and again O'Leary attempted a foray into the subject of literature. "A writer to be sure," he said, "and well named if I may say so." They shared a small laugh.

The big man looked out of place hunched over the steering wheel of the small car as he indulged in the odd habit of filling his cheeks with air and then blowing as though aggrieved by this or that remark. When, for example, the writer expressed an admiration for Joyce's story "The Dead," declaring it one of the best stories in the English language, O'Leary puffed out his cheeks and blew. "Well now, if it's the prose you're after, Joyce is your man and no mistake, Mr. Wright. But for playwriting, I'm inclined to Brendan Francis Behan. A good man with the words, he was. Dead now nearly ten years. Died from the drink they say, God rest his soul."

"Amen," said the novelist, adding, "An occupational hazard with writing."

"Is that a fact now, well, well." More puffing and blowing and a shift back to business.

"Sure, we'll get you a fine place to live, Mr. Wright. A fine home for the wife and little ones during your stay in our city."

But they didn't, and, after looking at yet another dingy apartment, he suggested to O'Leary that they move on, and with a huge puffing sigh the man agreed. This was hard and unrewarding work for both of them, and as the morning lengthened without success, their former genial conversation began to dwindle into merely polite replies. As he looked out at the streets, he could see only two categories of accommodation in Dublin: livable but hideously expensive or affordable and unlivable.

They went for lunch at a pub, O'Leary insisting that he

would look after things, but something within told the writer that the salesman was living on commission and paying his own way. When he said they could split the tab, O'Leary brightened. "As you wish, Mr. Wright."

They ate fish and chips and sank two pints of Guinness each, the strong brown beer reviving spirits, and O'Leary looked briefly hopeful, a look suggesting that a final cast of the reel might land this Canadian fish. But as the afternoon wore on, they both seemed to tire of one another. It was all too intense: the earlier amiable enthusiasm soaked now in disappointment on both sides. It was just not meant to be. Or so it seemed to him as he watched O'Leary turn the key to unlock another flat that was unsuitable. A heavy sigh. Then "I gather this one won't do either."

"I'm afraid not, Mr. O'Leary." He felt himself entering dangerous territory; he was now beginning to feel sorry for the man. Was he going to take one of these dumps for the summer just to make the man's day? One or two of them had not been not all that bad. They could probably manage, though he wouldn't look forward to his wife's assessment. And for a moment he thought of his father buying that ridiculous egg opener at the exhibition, the only artifact of his father's that he kept. He had left the medals and war souvenirs to others. He was sure his father had bought the damn thing because he felt sorry for the fellow. But that was a seventy-five-cent utensil. This was committing his family to a summer on a street they wouldn't like. He wouldn't do it, though he was interested in how the same kind of sympathy had come down that genetic highway. He wished his wife were with him. She would soon put a stop to any sentimental gestures. Then a moment's peevishness, which saved the day. In the car O'Leary said, "I have to say, sir, that given your circumstances and your budget as you called it, you can't afford to be too choosy. That last place now. With a little work, it would be perfectly fine for you. A little room all to yourself. For the writing. It could have worked." Almost at once he felt his sympathy for the man ebbing. If he was being too choosy about these high-priced Irish hovels, so what? It was his decision. All he wanted now was to get away from the salesman. He didn't care if O'Leary stopped the car and asked him to walk back to the hotel. He would find his own way. But they were now in someplace called Blackrock. Was this not where Donleavy's character Sebastian Dangerfield had once cavorted? All this looking for a place to live in Dublin was turning into nonsense, a hopeless case, which he thought a good title for a short story. But then hadn't Joyce called one of his stories "A Painful Case"? As they drove along, it seemed as if both of them were now alone with their thoughts, the day behind them in ruins. They returned to the hotel in silence, with O'Leary frowning, his salesman's cheery banter gone, his large ruddy face a study in frustration and probably concealed rage. They parted without a word, and he stood by the hotel and its doorman watching the little Ford merge into the traffic of O'Connell Street and feeling oddly bereft. He would like to have rented a flat from the man, but damn it to hell, none of them was worth the money.

He imagined Desmond O'Leary returning to his own flat having earned exactly nothing for the day's effort. Arriving home and heading for the bottle of Jameson on a shelf, taking the bottle and glass to the table and looking at his wife's back as she stood by the stove preparing his spuds and eggs, sensing his mood after an unlucky day. Still feeling obliged to offer support.

Common decency demanded that questions be asked. Without looking at him, sensing his silence and disappointment, she still asks the question they have both come to despise. "And how was your day then, Des?"

"Don't fecken ask, Kathleen."

"That bad, was it?"

"A fecken Canadian who called himself a writer and rattled on about fecken Joyce. Couldn't make up his mind. Nothing suited him. He should have stayed home, the silly bugger. Dragging his wife and kids here. It was plain as paint he couldn't afford to live in Dublin. A right fecken waste of a day it was. Do you want any of this? If not, I'm having another."

The next day they made plans to leave. The Irish trip had to be written off as a fiasco. But his wife had an idea. She'd been thinking about it in the night, guessing that he wouldn't find anything suitable they could afford in Dublin. She told him there was no use returning to Canada. All that money spent on airfare. They'd just look foolish. And where would they stay? At her parents'? At his? "Why don't I phone Mrs. Clutterbuck in Wootton," she said, "and see if Milford Bridge Cottage is available? We can spend the summer there. We enjoyed it so much last year. The kids loved it. You can write your TV play there." Because she wasn't "into" blame, she didn't hold his rash plan against him. She was into making the best of whatever situation was presented to them. He thought the place would probably be rented this late in the spring, but she said, "We won't know that unless we try, will we?" When the children heard, their six-year-old Christopher cheered, and his two-year-old brother, Andrew, clapped his hands, perhaps without knowing why.

To his delighted surprise, it worked out. When Phyllis

phoned, Mrs. Clutterbuck was happy to hear from her; she remembered how clean and tidy they had left it the previous year. Unfortunately, Milford Bridge was presently occupied by an Australian couple, but they were leaving in two weeks, so the Wrights were welcome to come for the rest of the summer on the same terms as the previous year. Phyllis agreed, and that evening they ate in the hotel dining room, an expensive meal but what the hell! They had Milford Bridge Cottage for the summer, and for the next two weeks they would find a bed and breakfast in Woodstock. They booked a flight to Bristol, where they rented a car and drove to Cirencester, a medieval town they liked with its ancient streets and cathedral. They stayed at a thirteenth-century tavern called the Sheep's Head and the next day drove to Woodstock and found a B & B near the gates to Blenheim Palace. Two weeks later they were settled again at Milford Bridge Cottage, where he set up his small writing room and began his play about a family in crisis after the father is diagnosed with terminal cancer. A happy home was being dismantled by misfortune. Wits were scattered and tempers short. A great deal of weeping and hand-wringing behind closed doors. The wife's name was Effie. Why? Or was that the grandmother? And what did it have to do with Henry James anyway? He was damned if he knew. He supposed he could always change the title.

Soldiering on with this travesty, he took solace only in the notion that as a writer he was put on earth to write only novels. He had once thought to write TV plays, but that was mere fancy. He knew writers who between books could perform more homely tasks like journalism or speech writing to pay the rent. But he abhorred that kind of writing. A year or two down the road during a particularly lean time a friend with connections in Ottawa would secure a writing job for him: a speech for a bureaucrat at Museums Canada. He was given a thick folder of material and a deadline. Deadlines always terrified him, brought out the dog in full cry. But he worked on that damn speech day and night for three weeks and mailed it off, seriously doubting that it would ever be delivered though he was paid handsomely. He wasn't, however, invited to write another, and that surely suggested something. Such as, he wasn't very good at it. As for his TV play, he sent it off without much hope of its ever being produced, and he was right. Somewhere in the bowels of the CBC's archives, it may lie stillborn. And a damn good thing too.

That summer his mind was often adrift in the little writing room at Milford Bridge Cottage as he thought of his second novel and how it would be received. Authors often think of their novels as children. When they are mature enough, the novelist sends them out into the world hoping they won't be too badly bruised by the rough justice of reviewers and critics. To his guarded amazement, however, things began to look promising. In a telegram his American publisher told him that *The New York Times* was interested in an interview. On his return from England, could he manage to come via New York? Yes, he could and gladly. A week later word arrived that *In the Middle of a Life* had been chosen as a Book-Of-The-Month Club selection for February. Oh, joy unbounded! Bring it on. He would endure.

They decided to take a week's holiday in the Lake District. Commune with the shade of that likeable old hophead Sam Coleridge and his sterner sometime friend, Will Wordsworth. He was intrigued by the relationship between the two men, polar opposites in temperament according to the biographies he was reading. There was Coleridge and his heroic struggle with depression and opium, often overwhelmed by loneliness and anxieties, dosing himself with laudanum, often puzzled and hurt by the harsh estrangement of the straitlaced Wordsworth, walking his pathways and hills with his long-legged gait.

At a hotel in Windermere with his family sleeping, he read the work of both poets late into the night, his mind often wandering to what lay ahead, the journey homeward with a stopover in New York "to meet the press." He pictured himself at a table in the bar of a fancy hotel.

When, years before, he ended his preaching and gave up his Bible readings at the age of fourteen, he lamented the absence of a deity whom he could thank for small favours or shake a fist at in exasperation. Some celestial Being who might offer a measure of comfort in affliction or punishment for shabby behaviour. But even then he realized that the only believable deity he could conjure up would be one who could not tolerate BS, who only smiled at mortals' vain hope for happiness in this life; in other words, a jokesmith who delighted in playing tricks on humans. And so in the midst of all that hope and happiness on their return from Windermere to Milford Bridge Cottage, a terse note from Roger Straus to say that *The New York Times* interview had been cancelled. Now why was that? he wondered. Had the idea for the interview originated in the critical acclaim of *The Weekend Man* and was this second novel now seen as a disappointment? Would the old jokesmith make him pay for a week's happiness? These foolish thoughts assailed him, and he now felt more apprehension about the second book. On the other hand, he said to himself in the dark of a sleepless night, listening to the little stream under Milford Bridge, there was absolutely nothing he could do about it now. He had written the book and it would soon be on its own, competing with hundreds of others.

In the meantime he was already thinking of another novel. Was this some kind of sickness, this willingness or desire to undertake something that he would have to devote the next two or three years to? His faith in his second novel had been slightly shaken by this note from New York, yet he was already experiencing a strange euphoria about the possibilities of another book. Was this not like an addict who has spent the week sweating out his addiction and now on Saturday night is pondering another fix as a reward for good behaviour? Oh yes, that feels better. It was true that in the initial stages of a new writing project the writer often finds a kind of home where he feels comforted and wanted, in fact needed. But surely, he thought, this is delusional. Sooner or later the book has to be judged in the real world and not in the writer's head. This time, however, he would get out from under the shadow of realism and write a long and funny account of a man's life, a bold and comic novel, a panoramic look at the follies and excesses of the entire twentieth century. No more domestic comedy. He would embrace the liberties of the picaresque. His models would be books by Swift and Sterne, and Henry Fielding. He had also read Thomas Berger's *Little Big Man* and John Barth's *The Sot-Weed Factor*. His next book then would skewer the ridiculous optimism of the century, reinforcing a beatitude dear to his heart. *Blessed is he who expects nothing, for he shall not be disappointed.* It would be a handbook for pessimists who laugh at the jests of Providence.

*

That fall he went on his first book tour and in Montreal had dinner with Mordecai Richler and his wife along with the poet John Glassco and Marion McCormack. Richler had been a strong supporter of *The Weekend Man* and along with Brian Moore the only Canadian writer to offer encouragement. He was always grateful for Richler's support, and they became, if not friends, mutually encouraging acquaintances. Meanwhile, *In the Middle of a Life* was receiving good reviews, especially in the UK, where it went on to win the Geoffrey Faber Memorial Prize, an award overshadowed now by the splashy Booker, but still estimable, as evidenced by such talented winners as Julian Barnes, Graham Swift and J. M. Coetzee. *In the Middle of a Life* also won the Toronto Book Award for fiction.

Following the tour he was glad to get back to his picaresque novel, *Farthing's Fortunes,* which chronicled the life of a ninety-year-old survivor, Billy Farthing, who gives his own version of the twentieth century's various follies. In its free-form style the picaresque has plenty of room for extravagant characters and bawdy humour, for coincidence and happenstance. He placed his eponymous narrator in an old folks' home from where he relates the main events of his extraordinary life beginning with the Klondike Gold Rush and moving on to the Great War, where he served in the British Army. Farthing was present at the Battle of the Somme on July 1, 1916, an infamous day in British military history when their army lost nearly sixty thousand men. On that day, Farthing was also wounded, a braining from an errant cricket ball, delivered in a staff officers' match well behind the lines, where Billy had stumbled on his mission to find Field Marshal Douglas Haig and murder him for his disastrous battle plan.

The blow to his head induced amnesia that lasted years, and he didn't regain consciousness until the onset of the Great Depression, when he was forced to ride the rails as a hobo with his erstwhile friend and mentor Cass Findlater, an American entrepreneur and swindler, an outsized character who embodies all the ruthless banditry of mercantile giants like Rockefeller and Morgan, forerunners of the corporate pirates who currently rule the Western world. *Farthing's Fortunes* was flawed perhaps by its excesses, but good-natured and fun to write. It was where he went each day in the mid-seventies to take his mind off money. He was still looking for a teaching job, but his applications to schools and colleges seemed to be gathering dust in filing cabinets. His experience was limited to that one semester at Lakefield College until he managed to get a teaching job at the Cobourg campus of Sir Sandford Fleming College, a weekly creative writing course for grown-ups. Every Tuesday night in that winter of 1974–75 he braved the icy terrors of Highway 28, driving from Peterborough down to the shores of Lake Ontario. Then in May 1975, he received a letter from Richard Bradley, headmaster of Ridley College in St. Catharines, Ontario, who didn't seem bothered by the applicant's slender academic credentials and lack of a teaching certificate; indeed, he appeared to be more interested that the applicant was a novelist; moreover, Bradley had already read both his novels.

By then he and Phyllis had finally got together enough money for a down payment on a house in Peterborough. According to curious neighbours who watched their arrival, the previous tenants had been members of a motorcycle gang, and evidence of their occupancy was everywhere. The large brick house on Frederick Street would need considerable work. There were tire tracks from motorcycles in the living room; apparently the police had been regular visitors on Saturday nights.

The neighbours were delighted to see a young family now living in the big corner house. But after the rampages of the barbarians, it took a great deal of effort to make the place habitable. This work was onerous, but flaws aside, after nine years of living in rented apartments and cottages, they were grateful and happy to call it home, enjoying those early weeks of happiness experienced by first-time owners. Much of the work fell to his wife, who could in fact hammer a nail with more authority than he could. He tried his hand at painting and was given a passing grade. Mostly he followed her directions, and soon the house began to take shape.

Because they had lived all their married lives in rented accommodation, they had very little furniture, and they were now living in a big empty house with only four chairs and a kitchen table. The rest of it would have to be makeshift until they got settled. The letter from Bradley indicating interest was followed by a phone call on a Saturday. He said he was visiting Trinity College School in Port Hope and could he come around on the next day for a visit? Well, why not? And why not have dinner too? He guessed they would be on display, assessed as potential members of the Ridley community. They had a day to prepare. After the motorcycle tracks were erased and the general squalor cleaned up, the living room didn't look half bad. There was a large handsome fireplace, from which perhaps the bikers had lit their bongs, managing somehow not to burn down the place. There was no dining room, so they improvised. With not a table in the house worthy of the name, they made do with an old door found in the basement. This was supported by two sawhorses from the garage and covered with a large clean white bedsheet. In the flickering lights of candle and hearth, it would work. The kitchen chairs were dusted off.

He was counting on his guest not being a teetotaller and so laid in a bottle of Chianti sitting in its little wicker basket on the white bedsheet. And in case the visitor needed to clear his throat after the drive up, they bought a bottle of Cutty Sark. These provisions would be much appreciated by one and all. A few books then on the mantel to advertise the household's belief in literature as a civilizing force in a rude world and Bob's your uncle, as they used to say in the King's Head in Wootton, Oxfordshire.

The next day Richard Bradley, an amiable ruddy-faced Englishman in his fifties with the solid bearing of a former rugby player, arrived. The headmaster was surprisingly down-to-earth, with a sense of humour and a great love of literature, Scotch, wine and good food, all of which they enjoyed that evening. They talked about favorite writers, and shared a view of the importance of literature in the education of young people. Many years later he told Bradley about their preparations for that dinner and asked if he'd noticed the makeshift table with its door and a sawhorse legs. Would he have cared? "Not a bit," he said. He knew enough about writers to surmise that they were usually short on funds and didn't live in castles. He said he remembered only the good conversation among the three of them.

On that evening Bradley sounded him out on what to expect as a schoolmaster. He was careful to warn him that life in a boarding school was busy, even hectic at times. Masters, as teachers were called, not only were expected to teach their classes but also were assigned to houses for house duty once a week to relieve the housemaster. He should expect as well a weekend house duty each term. There was also dining house duty and the coaching of a sport or extracurricular activity for two of the three terms. That didn't leave much time for writing, and how did he feel about that? But all he could think of as he listened was that he would have a cheque coming in every fortnight. The regularity of a salary, a pension plan, health insurance for his family was irresistible. He said that he'd thought about all that and concluded that he could live with it. There was always the summer for writing. This he said had been always their plan. Eventually Phyllis wanted to go to university and begin a career of her own. They had worked hard for all this and he wasn't under any illusions that life in a school like Ridley would be easy. But even with only his limited experience at Lakefield and Cobourg, he knew he would enjoy teaching. When they said good night at the front door, Bradley told him he would be in touch within a few days. A week later the headmaster phoned to say that, if he were still interested, there was a job for him in the English Department at Ridley College, and he accepted the offer. Now he would have a steady income at last.

A week later as a family they visited, and the boys, now four and eight, were excited each in his own way and eager to become a part of the big imposing school with its manicured lawns and hedges, its playing fields and swimming pool, its hockey rink, the well-kept buildings, the Great Hall. His wife could now begin to plan a career outside the home. Was this not how most people lived? No more worrying half the night about whether or not the clutch on the VW was nearly finished. Was it not silly to lie awake at night worrying about the cost of a new clutch? Of course it was. But then when he thought of it, most things that kept anxiety-stricken people awake in the night were ridiculous. But try telling that to such people at three o'clock in the morning. Anxious people, he knew, cling to their fears and become addicted to worry. After several years at the top of the list, his worries about money had been banished.

He knew he would have other things to fret about, foremost among them, his uncertainty at entering this strange new world. What did he really know about private schools anyway? The boys he had taught at Lakefield College that semester were intelligent and polite, but what was most impressive about them was their social poise, their confidence and ease in adult company. Where had they learned that? At school? They appeared to have none of the doubts and uncertainties that had afflicted him when he was their age. Were Lakefield boys snobbish? He hadn't thought so, and he had no reason to believe that Ridley students would be any different.

Perhaps his most negative view of private school boys came from his childhood, when he and his friends in their short pants and faded tee shirts, their sockless, stinky feet in worn running shoes, would hang around the town dock in Midland waiting for the big passenger ships with their American tourists who sometimes threw money at them. On those summer afternoons long ago, a train from Toronto would also come into the dock, and one day he watched a group of schoolboys disembark. They looked clean and were smartly dressed in shirts and pressed shorts and polished black shoes. The younger ones wore ties and beanies and were herded together by the older boys and teachers. The group cast barely a glance at the town boys while they lined up dutifully to board the steamer that would take them to a camp on an island further up the bay. At the time he thought those boys looked full of themselves, too big for their britches as his mother might have said. But years later he would come to realize that his impression was probably nothing more than reverse snobbery, a working-class resentment of those with money and privilege who merely by their presence exert a confidence he both hated and envied.

At Ridley he was soon enjoying the experience of teaching both boys and girls for in 1973, under Bradley's enlightened stewardship, Ridley College had become the first boys' boarding school in Canada to admit female students. In 1975, when he joined the faculty, there were still very few girls, but in the years ahead their numbers would increase to equal the boys, and he was delighted because, by and large, girls seemed to enjoy and excel in English more than most boys. From that first year, with the help of George Orwell's words and those of Strunk and White's *The Elements of Style,* he was determined to teach his students how to write clean and concise sentences, emphasizing the need to avoid clichés, euphemisms and weasel words, a term some of them came to love. The Ministry of Education's course outline that year was a useful text, with its sundry examples of pretentious jargon. Sometimes he challenged his students by giving them particularly opaque passages to clarify. Because he had no teaching certificate, his classes were never visited by a ministry inspector, though he often wished that one would drop by, for he would have enjoyed demonstrating how that government document was a handy source of bad writing habits that with a little attention could be made, at the very least, understandable.

As Bradley had warned him, life in a boarding school was

exceedingly busy, and sometimes he felt overwhelmed by how intrusive that life could be; at parties and dinners conversation was almost always about what was happening at the school. Life beyond the gates didn't seem to interest many of his colleagues. Sometimes he had to convince himself that he was there to make a living, not a life, but he began to wonder if that was possible or even desirable. Perhaps a satisfying life in a boarding school was rather like one in a religious order, achievable only through total commitment. In any event his life was about to become much busier, because in February 1976 the head of the English Department decided to accept an offer from Upper Canada College, and Bradley asked the writer to assume the headship of the department at the end of the school year. With only five months of teaching experience, he was surprised but also flattered and so took it on. He reasoned perhaps that since his third novel, *Farthing's Fortunes,* had already been accepted by Atheneum in New York and Macmillan in Toronto he was in no hurry to juggle writing with teaching; he would concentrate on the job they were paying him to do. But in his heart he knew that one day he would somehow have to find time to write, that his life would not be complete unless he had a story to tell and the time to tell it.

Over the next few years, finding a balance between teaching and writing would be a struggle, and he would come to regret his decision to accept the headship of the department, with its meetings and seemingly endless administrative chores. But this all came, he reminded himself, with something called a salary. Had he forgotten that? Well yes, perhaps he had now and again, because his journal entries throughout the 1970s read like an endless litany of complaint about "durance vile" at the school.

Reading them many years later, he could only shake his head in disbelief and one evening said to his wife, "My God, I whined an awful lot about how much I had to do at Ridley back in the seventies."

She laughed. "No kidding. Tell me about it. But wait. Don't bother. I was there, remember?"

So she was. As for his faulty memory, had he also forgotten how wonderful it was at the end of the school year—after all the marking of examinations and the grades entered and the promotion meetings over—to anticipate the ten weeks of freedom ahead: the car trip to Gaspé with overnights at Auberge du Faubourg in St-Jean-Port-Joli or Les Gouverneurs at Rimouski? A month to be refreshed by the air and the sea and the countryside? Had he forgotten that? No, he hadn't. "Seal my lips if ever I say another bad word about boarding school life!" These remarks were met by yet another brief burst of laughter. From both of them.

Treading Water

In the late fall of 1976 his third novel was first received with an excellent advance review in *Publishers Weekly*, and the headmaster came by their house one Sunday morning and dropped off a copy of *The New York Times*, with its positive half-page review. But of course there were other opinions of his tale. An obtuse review from William French in *The Globe and Mail* defied description, reminding him of a story about a German physicist who said of a colleague's paper on some arcane subject, "This isn't right. It isn't even wrong." But the book had its supporters, and he received a good deal of mail about it. In those days if readers wanted to get in touch with an author, they had to write a letter: they had to think for more than ten seconds about what they wanted to say, use more than a hundred and forty characters, and then they had to put the letter into an envelope, attach a stamp and slip it into a mailbox. How tedious, many might think today, though no one thought so then, and there were advantages to this archaic means of communicating, the foremost being that the letter writer could not so easily hide in the dark thickets of anonymity, his name signifying responsibility for his opinions. He answered all the letters. A professor from somewhere in Ohio—or was it Indiana?—was so taken with Billy Farthing, Sally Bliss, Findlater and the whole cast that he used the book in his classroom as some kind of commentary on the twentieth century.

In fact, he received a great deal of mail from those who enjoyed his panoramic look and send-up of so-called progress in a century riven by wars, greed and foolishness, though in retrospect he supposed that this was true of almost any century in human history. Meantime, he was still trying to adjust to the routines and strictures of boarding school life, measuring out his life not with Prufrock's coffee spoons but with the bells that jangled his nerves when they rang for classes.

> *There is something monstrous*
> *about bells ringing*
> *Every forty minutes.*
> *Quartering my mornings*
> *And afternoons.*
> *I say "Balls to bells."*

All right, he was no poet, but at least the words identified an attitude though not a particularly good one to carry around the school. He was trying to find some time to write, and years later, looking at his journals for that time, he can see that he started but never finished stories. In the summer of 1977 he was trying to write a screenplay of his latest novel. A kind of madness must have gripped him in those days. Dreams of fortunes made in Hollywood. Had he not read the dismal evidence of failure by writers who had tried their hands at this? Yes, he had, and still he carried this hopeless script to Gaspé on their annual holiday. He should have been taking some serious medication for those hallucinations. And what was this barely legible and surely drunken scrawl composed no doubt in the dead hours of New Year's Eve when the revels had ended and he was alone with his thoughts?

And so another year. Materially well off and healthy all four of us. But as for writing, sweet bugger all! Still let us count our blessings and say goodnight.

Two weeks later on a Sunday night, his sister-in-law in Midland phoned to tell him that his father had died two hours earlier, stricken by a heart attack. He had eaten dinner at his eldest son's house and then with his wife walked the two blocks to his home. It was a cold night, and that may have caused havoc with his angina, for when he stepped through the doorway of his warm house, he collapsed: dead, the doctor later surmised, before he hit the floor. Not a bad way to go a month from his eighty-first birthday, but hard on his wife, who was horrified by this sudden and startling end of the man with whom she had shared fifty-four years of life. His father, born near the end of the nineteenth century, had lived to see the invention of electric light, the automobile, airplane, radio and television, technological wonders he could not have imagined as a small child on a farm in rural Ontario. It was hardly surprising then that in the early days of television he sat watching the Indian Head test pattern waiting for the six o'clock news with its pictures in his living room. A quiet man, he had endured and survived a calamitous war, and afterwards raised a large family on not much money, a man who left this life with as little fuss as he made throughout his eighty years on the planet. Looking at him a few days later in his casket at the funeral home, surrounded by old Legion friends and fellow workers from the elevator, his youngest son remembered the snow-filled mornings and his shovelling, with his father coming out of the house, pulling down the earflaps of his cap and tucking the lunch pail under his arm, shaking his head at the boy but offering an indulgent smile. "Just a narrow path through to the street, Son. That's all I need. You can always come back and fix it later. Okay?" Then pushing through the waist-high snow.

At the funeral home another memory surfaced. A summer evening and his father standing at a window staring out at a storm-laden sky where now and then lightning flickered through the clouds and thunder rumbled. Looking at his father that evening, he wondered if he was thinking of another time long ago and the beginning of a barrage. His father never talked much about the old War. Like many veterans he kept his memories to himself, thinking that perhaps it was all best left unspoken. Yet after he'd read his son's account of the Battle of the Somme in *Farthing's Fortunes,* he talked briefly about an episode in his life as a soldier. At the time, he said, he was a runner. Listening to the story, it was sometimes hard for him to believe that his father had lived at a time when communication on a battlefield was essentially the same as it had been on the plains of Marathon in Greece nearly five hundred years before the birth of Christ. A message was carried inside the tunic of a man with strong legs and steady nerves from a position behind the lines, perhaps a battalion's headquarters, to a trench or dugout closer to the front; the soldier ran through the darkness across a field torn apart by old battles with its shell holes, blasted strands of barbed wire, scampering rats and the rotting bodies of horses, the runner hoping and likely praying that he would not be caught in a barrage. Then after delivering the message he returned with the field commander's reply. This was the runner's job.

On that particular night, after handing over the message, he was offered a cup of tea in the dugout. Another soldier frying pancakes asked if he'd like some. He surely would, but the tea had gone right through him and he needed a leak. He'd be back in a few minutes. After climbing the ladder he stood a few yards behind the dugout entrance and just then a whiz-bang exploded above his head. Whiz-bangs, his father told him, were devilishly frightening shells that exploded almost without warning.

"You heard this whizzing sound, and then a bang that could deafen you. It just scared the dickens out of you. Actually they scared you more than anything else because you thought they were so close though they might not have been."

But then another, much larger shell burst over the entrance to the dugout, knocking him backwards, and he lay there in his sodden pants waiting for the next one. But it fell to one side and further away. He learned later that everyone in the dugout had been killed.

After listening to his father's story he said, "So if you hadn't needed to take a leak, you and I wouldn't be here talking to one another sixty years later. We're alive because of that tea and your full bladder that night."

His father was again looking out at the sky and the teeming rain. "Yes," he said, "I suppose you could say that, though it seems an odd way to look at things."

"Well, Dad," he said, "I'm an odd fellow."

His father laughed. "Yes," he said quietly, still looking out at the rain, "I suppose you are, but that's okay."

The author's father somewhere in France in 1917 at the age of twenty.

*

In the summer of 1977 he had been horrified by that most vile of crimes, the rape and murder of a child in Toronto. The victim was a twelve-year-old boy named Emanuel Jaques, the son of Portuguese immigrants from the Azores. At the time, downtown Toronto, particularly the east side of Yonge Street between Dundas and Gerrard Streets, was a sordid farrago of strip bars, porn shops and body rub parlours. Drugs were readily available on the street where Emanuel and his friends worked daily shining shoes. One afternoon the boy was lured away by the promise of money for his help in selling stolen cameras and was eventually abducted by four men. They kept the boy in an apartment above a body rub parlour where he was repeatedly sodomized before being strangled and drowned in a kitchen sink, his body hidden under a pile of wood on the roof of the building. The murderers were eventually captured and sent to prison for life, but many people were outraged by the brutal reality of such a crime in their city.

He too was shaken by the child's debasement and murder. It was a parent's worst nightmare, and, like many other fathers on those hot summer days, he found himself looking carefully at his ten- and six-year-old sons, trying hard to eliminate the images of Emanuel's last day on earth, the pain and suffering of his final hours. After the murderers had finished with the boy, they drowned him; and in his imagination he saw one holding on to the boy's thrashing legs while another held his head in the sink. It was all in his imagination, but still it was there and almost too horrible to picture. Even thinking about it left him trembling with fear and rage. Could he find the words to describe the depravity of the crime or the anguish of a parent who must then live with that memory for the rest of his life? It haunted him, even in dreams—that twelve-year-old boy's terrible death— and he knew that he would have to imagine his way into a story about a boy and his father and a murderer. Already in some dark corner of his mind he carried the words of the book's opening sentence, *When, after an hour, Farris's twelve-year-old son did not return to the apartment, the man began to worry.*

During this time he had begun and abandoned two novels, increasingly frustrated by his failure to juggle teaching and writing. He and Phyllis talked about all this. She would be graduating from Niagara College as a library technician at the end of June 1979, and she was optimistic about finding a job. In November 1978 he had told the headmaster that he would be leaving Ridley the following June, at the end of the school year. He vowed to himself that at the beginning of January 1979, he would devote the first two hours of every day to this new novel. Those two hours would be sacrosanct, inviolable. No skipping a day. The payoff would be in words. Even half a page of words was worth getting up for. Had he not read that Graham Greene settled for only six hundred words a day? It would be difficult but not impossible, and, once started, there would be the satisfaction in knowing that he had another life, a secret life far beyond the classroom. Surely that would embolden him on rough days.

In August 1979 they moved to a house on St. Patrick Street. By then he had finished the first draft; the story was told, at least to himself. He finished the second draft in October and by November had submitted the manuscript to Douglas Gibson at Macmillan of Canada and Charles Corn, who was now chief editor at Dutton in New York. Both liked the novel, and soon Macmillan in London agreed to publish too. He felt relieved, grateful to have completed it. Writing the book had expunged his rage and fears. Drained the poison from his imagination.

That spring Macmillan had been bought by the educational

publisher Gage, who apparently coveted the Macmillan trade list, which included his new novel, *Final Things,* scheduled for publication that fall. His first contact with the new owners was a letter from Mr. W———, who identified himself as vice-president and general manager.

Macmillan of Canada
A Canadian Company
The Macmillan Company of Canada Limited
70 Bond Street, Toronto, Ontario M5B 1X3
Telex 06-22324   Tel. (416) 362-7651

May 30, 1980

REGISTERED MAIL

Mr. Richard Wright
52 St. Patrick Street
St. Catharines, Ontario
L2R 1K3

Dear Mr. Wright:

ANDREW TOLLIVER - BB #11
FARTHINGS FORTUNES
WEEKEND MAN - LL #57

I am sorry to have to tell you that annual sales of your books have diminished to a point where we find it necessary to allow them to go out of print.

In accordance with the terms of our contracts for the publication of these books, formal notice is hereby given (i) that we wish to discontinue their publication effective September 1, 1980, and (ii) that effective December 1, 1980, we propose to dispose of any remaining copies as we see fit and to account to you for any sales in accordance with the terms of the contracts. I suggest that you refer to the contracts for further details on matters such as copyright status.

I regret this necessity. We are pleased to have been your publishers and have valued our association with you.

This was not a propitious beginning.

In late September he and his wife went to England for two weeks. And on their return he confronted the reviews of *Final Things.* Many were positive, admiring the honesty and craftsmanship of the book. Some complained that it was depressing. But how could the death of a child not be depressing? In late December movie rights for *Final Things* was optioned by

52 st. Patrick Street
St. Catharines,Ontario
June 3,1980

Dear Mr. W____:
            Thank you for your letter of May 30 informing
me that three of my books - Andrew Tolliver , Farthing's Fortunes
and The Weekend Man will shortly be going out of print. This
news is regretable,but perhaps understandable,though I think you
are making a serious mistake with the paper edition of The Weekend
Man.

            What I don't find understandable,however, is the
last sentence of your letter(We are pleased to have been your
publisher and have valued our association with you.). This
strikes me as a peculiarly tactless and inane way of addressing
an author who in fact will be publishing a new book with your
firm this Fall.

                        Yours sincerely,

                        Richard B. Wright

c.c. Douglas Gibson
      Georges Borchardt

a Canadian company. Option money was always useful, but in his life as a writer he never took any talk of movies based on his books seriously.

*

For him the 1980s will be forever remembered as the nadir of his writing life, a period of unrest and uncertainty. The inflationary seventies now had to be paid for, and everything was tightened in that age of Reagan and Thatcher and Mulroney. The country was in recession and unemployment was high. They were not broke, and he knew they would survive; his wife was working and also taking courses toward a degree that would eventually lead to an impressive and satisfying career as an academic librarian. But that was several years away. He was making a little money, but he felt uninspired and stalled. He had quickly written another novel, *The Teacher's Daughter,* a somewhat melodramatic account of an affair between a thirty-six-year-old schoolteacher, Janice Harper, and a young tough, James Hicks. Any sensible author has doubts during the writing of a book, but such apprehension can usually be offset by good days when the story's words seem to fall into place. But rereading his journal entries for that year, he was not surprised to discover a persistent uneasiness with both the tale and the telling of it.

Douglas Gibson at Macmillan, however, liked the book well enough and wanted only a few minor changes. But in New York the writer's agent Georges Borchardt could find no takers. Meantime he thought of writing a thriller, a book that might make some serious money. It was either that or paid employment. At the urging of a former colleague he had an interview with Ridley's new headmaster, Jeremy Packard, during which he talked about the possibility of returning to teaching. Packard said he would keep him in mind. *The Teacher's Daughter* was published in 1982, and to his surprise *The Globe and Mail* review was positive and so were many others. The book also attracted another film option, this time from the National Film Board, where he met the Montreal writer Bill Weintraub, who counted himself among the novel's admirers. He and Bill spent a fruitless but delightful day in the wilds of Scarborough, scouting possible sites for film scenes.

At the beginning of that year he and Kildare Dobbs had escaped the January blues with a week in Mexico, where they stayed in a cheap tourist hotel in Cozumel, escaping injury and possible death one afternoon following a bibulous lunch when Kildare, approaching a sharp curve, steered their motor scooter into a roadside bush of bougainvillea. There they lay unhurt amid the colourful flowers, delirious with the laughter that usually arrives after a close encounter with harm. That holiday would provide the setting for his next book, *Tourists,* a comic adventure in which an agreeable couple from Nebraska whom he and Dobbs actually met on this trip were transmogrified into a hideous duo who tormented the story's narrator, a nervous and shy schoolmaster unused to being away from home. Judging by his mail, many readers loved this black comedy, and it found publishers in both New York and London. Yet he began to sense that he was writing in a hurry and with less care, eager perhaps to score a hit, always a dangerous strategy for a mid-list writer. Even his agent Georges Borchardt agreed and in a letter wrote, "I think you are writing outside yourself." It was, he thought, an apposite observation.

Oddly enough he began to consider the notion that he would be better off mentally and in many other ways if he returned to teaching. *Write less but write better.* What was the hurry anyway? Besides, he missed teaching. It was true that boarding school life was busy and always would be. But a great deal of the busyness he'd experienced in the seventies had stemmed from being thrust into that headship only months after he started teaching. He was never given time to catch his breath. If he could now just teach? In March 1981 he spent two weeks at Ridley filling in for a teacher who had to take over administrative duties because of another's illness; he found the experience an agreeable change from his daily wrestle with words and the blank page. Perhaps writing by itself was *not* the very best way for him; maybe after his morning's work (for he couldn't write all day) he had too much time to brood and worry about where it was all taking him. Or not taking him. By the end of 1984 he felt burnt out and thoroughly discouraged. So when he heard that Ridley would soon be looking for an English teacher, he was ready. And when they called him, he again accepted the job.

He had gone astray, that old word he remembered from his luncheon conversation with Harry Painter in the Savarin restaurant twenty-five years ago. He had to remember that a serious writer was interested not just in providing entertainment but also in using the power of language to understand experience. He would try to remember that and write fewer books of better quality. The old original plan from the 1960s—write and teach—was still worth pursuing.

His return to the classroom in September 1985 was an opportunity for renewal. He had spent the summer carefully preparing; he would put any thoughts of another novel "on hold" and devote himself to his classes and his pastoral responsibilities, so again he entered into boarding school life and was welcomed by old friends. He came to enjoy teaching the students, and they seemed to like his passion for narrative and language, his insistence on the value of clarity. He taught the work of writers he had loved and learned from, the prose and poetry that had informed his own passion for literature. His students read Shakespeare and Chaucer, Conrad and Alice Munro, and Albert Camus, whose novel *The Outsider* he had read in a country cemetery one autumn in 1959.

In June 1987 he spent three weeks at the Leighton Artists' Colony in Banff, Alberta, trying to write a short story—a change of scenery, a change of narrative pace—and he thought it might work. But he was never comfortable with the short story; he seemed to need the more expansive architecture of the novel, and so the story he was writing, "Miss Ormsby's Revolt," morphed into his seventh novel, *Sunset Manor,* the exploration of life in a retirement home as experienced by a feisty spinster who is not comfortable with group activities and manufactured cheer. Published by Seal Books in the spring of 1990, it received a mixed reception and had only modest sales. Oddly enough, in time it was published in Japan, largely he imagined because that country had a ready supply of elderly folk who wanted stories about people much like themselves. It was pleasing to think of his books finding readers in distant lands. By the end of his writing life his novels had appeared in many countries.

Barachois, Gaspé—Haymaking—
Taking a beer break at Uncle Isaac's.

They spent their summers in Barachois on the Gaspé coast, where as a young man he had written his first novel in the late sixties, and it was there at the age of fifty-four that he looked within himself and at his life with words. Had he quite simply run out of gas? He can still remember walking along the deserted beach wondering in what direction his writing might now take him. Or would it take him anywhere? He surely wouldn't be the first to offer a shrug and tell himself that he had done his best. Now perhaps it was time to call it a day. Such a prospect even promised a kind of peace from the spirals of anxiety and depression that inevitably accompanied his writing. Could he not accept the brutal reality that publishers were seldom interested in middle-aged writers whose backlists were out of print? At one point he had received a royalty cheque for $2.85. Was it really so bad to say "that's enough." Wouldn't words still be there in his teaching life? At the same time he had to wonder if writing was by now so much a part of him that he would feel lost without it. Suppose he just ignored all the business about his out of print backlist, his current fallowness, his worries about whether or not editors would like what he wrote. Why not just write something for the sheer pleasure of using words, to write a story he felt like telling? A book probably no one would publish. The pleasure would lie solely in the telling. And, oh, Christ! Was that the red dog coming out from behind some bushes down the beach, stretching and yawning? Beginning its trot toward him. He fancied the little devil was grinning, pleased with himself at the thought of another trip with the writing man. Eager as ever to be a nuisance by the bedside at night. Just as he had been on all the other journeys through the man's fiction. More important, however, the writer realized that he was just kidding himself if he thought he could write a book solely for his own pleasure, saying, "It won't matter if this doesn't work out." He knew otherwise; it matters all right. It's everything or damn close to it, and if he didn't feel that way about it—if writing a book just became a retirement hobby, something just to fill the time between now and Nothing—then he was telling lies to himself. Because ahead of him for the next couple of years would be the story he had to tell at this point in his life, and he would have to live again with whatever accompanied it, including the dog's company.

The Age of Longing

Soon he would be spending afternoons in Brock University Library lost in the microfilm of old newspapers chronicling the 1930s, watching the world unfurl its banners of dismal news from what the poet W. H. Auden famously called "a low dishonest decade." What was it that attracted him to that period? He remembered none of it. He was born toward its end and grew up in the war years of the 1940s. But, in fact, in that childhood he had been surrounded by the artifacts of the previous decade. During World War II, the manufacture of most domestic goods was put on hold as industrial North America transformed itself into a heavy supplier of munitions and armour for "the war effort." This American-driven industrial production did as much as anything to ensure an Allied victory in 1945. But it also meant that while people then emerging from the Great Depression had money in their pockets, there was little to buy in the way of new goods: no cars, no refrigerators, no new housing. People drove automobiles that had come off assembly lines ten or fifteen or twenty years before. In the summers they still used iceboxes to preserve their food and in winter crossed their fingers and coaxed another year out of old furnaces and hot water heaters. A household in 1944 would not have looked much different from one in 1935. And despite the war, the 1930s with its unemployment and hardships, its door-to-door tramps looking for handouts, was still, for many, an open wound, a bad memory, a place they had escaped from but were still haunted by. His parents and their friends still talked about it, and these struggles would become an important narrative in his childhood. Now, a half century later, he wanted to explore the lives of ordinary people during that time.

Placing his characters in the middle of the decade—1935—he set his story in Huron Falls, a fictional version of his hometown. His two main characters were unlikely partners, and he would have to make their marriage plausible: Buddy Wheeler, a good-looking, unambitious but talented hockey player who grew up in a rough part of town, and Grace Stewart, a daughter of the manse, a disciplined and severe young woman, an elementary schoolteacher, a precursor of the eponymous narrator of his next novel, *Clara Callan*.

Thinking and feeling his way into this book, which was originally called *Presbyterian Blues*, he read accounts of life in the thirties, and after a while began to feel and sense those times: the smell of furniture polish and old wax on seldom-used parlour floors, the yellow light through the tasseled lampshades under which were read the novels of Pearl Buck and Thomas Wolfe; the boxy floor-model radios with their big glowing dials, where from behind the cloth-covered speakers came the voices of characters from *Ma Perkins* and *Pepper Young's Family, The Shadow* and *Boston Blackie.* He could smell the wood and coal smoke from chimneys on winter nights when men in overcoats and homburgs or fedoras and boys in fur-trimmed caps tramped along snowy streets to hockey games at the Arena Gardens, where their local hero Buddy Wheeler would dazzle them with his stick handling, and speed, his famous backhand goals.

He would tell his story in the voice of Howard Wheeler, an editor in a publishing company in Toronto who now, in middle age, is intrigued by the early years of his parents' unlikely courting and marriage. How did all that come about? How did a serious-minded young woman like Grace Stewart marry a man as feckless as Buddy Wheeler? They were so different both temperamentally and culturally, and the marriage was over by the time Howard was a young boy. And so the mysteries surrounding his parents were still out there to be explored. It all seemed so unlikely. And yet such marriages did happen, not only in fiction, but also in fact.

Again he would fit the writing of a novel into his schedule at the school. Again he would get used to getting up at 4:30 or 5:00 and taking a glass of cold water down to his writing desk in the basement. Some days he felt like pouring the water over his head to induce full wakefulness. This routine varied only if it were a morning following house duty, when he often didn't get home until after eleven o'clock. An austere schedule, the sacrificial austerity creeping into his sense of worth. He used to think that perhaps medieval monks felt this way: measuring their goodness by their sacrifice, their rigorous denial of a full night's sleep. Certainly on a day when he managed two good pages, it was hard not to feel just a little ahead of his fellow human beings for that morning at least. At the end of the school year, he would adjust to a more leisurely pace that would include the whole morning.

Curiously enough there were no notes on the novel's progress that year in his journal until the late fall, when he recorded the discovery of an epigraph for his book from an essay entitled "What Is Style?" in Mavis Gallant's *Paris Notebooks*.

> *Against the sustained tick of a watch, fiction takes the measure of a life, a season, a look exchanged, the turning point, desire as brief as a dream, the grief and terror that after childhood we cease to express. The lie, the look, the grief are without permanence. The watch continues to tick where the story stops.*

He had met Gallant through a mutual friend, Tess Taconis, formerly Tess Boudreau, sister of Mordecai Richler's first wife. He liked Mavis's forthrightness and, in her impatience with nonsense, her hard-to-please nature, sensed a kindred spirit. She was then writer-in-residence at the University of Toronto, and two or three times that year he travelled to the city for lunch with her. Geography would keep them from seeing too much of one another, but later in his life when he and Phyllis would visit Paris, they always arranged a dinner with Mavis at one of her favourite restaurants in Montparnasse.

By the beginning of 1993, he had nearly finished the first draft of his eighth novel, and in the middle of that month he began the rewrite, only to be stopped cold by a Monday morning call from his wife, who happened to be home that day. She had just heard from his sister-in-law in Midland; his mother's kidneys were failing, and according to the doctor it didn't look good. The day before she had been admitted to the hospital suffering from a bowel obstruction accompanied by mild pneumonia. She was now in her eighty-ninth year, and he had to wonder if this all signaled the beginning of the end. That morning he alerted his department head and hastily left the school for home, where he packed a bag. He can remember thinking how quickly superstition clings to consciousness when death draws near. Would taking his only suit be unlucky? Would the anticipation of her funeral hasten her death? He must have given his head a shake, for he had always rejected the notion that events can be influenced by knocking on wood or packing a suit for a funeral before death was officially announced. He badly wanted to see his mother before she died, anxious now to tell her how much she had meant to him, how close in temperament they were, how much he cherished the childhood she had given him. If she could just hold on until he got there with his words of gratitude. Placing the suit bag in the car trunk, he left for the drive northward, stopping only in Oakville to pick up his sister.

In Midland they went directly to the hospital, arriving just before noon and, according to a nurse, only ten minutes or so after their mother had "passed away." He frowned at the euphemism he'd always despised for its sentimental avoidance of a perfectly good word for the end of life. His mother was still in the narrow bed she had died in, and they were allowed to enter the room where she lay, now a mere facsimile of her small self, a frail body under hospital sheets, one yellowing eye still visible beneath a half-closed lid. Beside him his sister wept while he touched his mother's face, afraid to close that partly opened eye lest he do some damage. Let others who know the trade attend the dead.

After the death of parents we make our own grim calculations; now orphans in middle age we consider, if only briefly, the time remaining to us; putting aside accidents and misadventures, we wonder how much time we might have left. He was nearly fifty-six and seriously doubted whether he would be around for another thirty-two years like his mother. She had unwittingly led a healthy life, scarcely touching alcohol, only reluctantly accepting, on special occasions, "perhaps a small glass of ale"; the memory of that phrase making him smile at how her words magically transformed a common glass of beer into something that to her at least must have sounded more refined. In the 1940s and 1950s she smoked cigarettes, but sparingly, only two or three Matinées a week and always in her home. Now and then she could be persuaded by him to share an Old Gold or Lucky Strike from one of the cartons, not too cleverly concealed in the closet of the boys' bedroom, cigarettes that had been smuggled home by his brothers from the American ports where their boats had docked. He and his mother never used the word *stealing*. She might say, "I'm sure they won't miss one package." He never smoked a Lucky Strike without remembering the radio commercials, the sound of Morse code and a deeply authoritative voice announcing the letters and words. L.S.M.F.T. Lucky Strike Means Fine Tobacco. As horny adolescents he and his friends and doubtless thousands of other teenagers had mocked the pompous slogan with "L.S.M.F.T. Let's Screw, My Finger's Tired."

All this he remembered at the funeral, looking down with a

wry smile one last time at the small face in the coffin, the words so arranged in his memory they had turned grief into salacious adolescent humour, remembering too how she had once objected to the profanity in one of his novels, which she probably caught only in a glance at the book. He doubted that she had read any of his work from beginning to end.

"You shouldn't use such words," she said.

And what had he replied? "Those aren't my words, Ma. They belong to the character in the book."

Shameless sophistry and he knew it and so probably did she though she wouldn't have recognized the word *sophistry*. But she had given him that old familiar look which he knew spelled *smart alec*.

*

He needed to get away, not only from the grief surrounding his mother's death but also from the novel that was so stubbornly resisting him that winter. In March they went to Italy for two weeks, and there, amid the splendours of Venice and Florence and Siena, he felt refreshed by the compelling otherness of an old culture. Upon their return, he felt restored, the book moving slowly forward, though as always he was beset by doubts, recording his dismay that summer in Gaspé.

Thursday, July 29—Could only manage one page and then this afternoon overwhelmed by crippling depression about this book. I should expect these bleak moments by now for they've arrived during every book I've written. But Christ Almighty, where do they come from and why? Just my bloody nature, I suppose.

Yet six weeks later he wrote,

Thursday, September 9—Finished my novel today at 5:00 P.M.

After carefully going over it two more times, he gave it to his wife to proofread, and she then transferred his words to the computer, and he sent the manuscript to his new agent in Toronto, Janet Turnbull. She got back to him within a couple of days expressing enormous enthusiasm for the book, though she didn't like the title. That was all right because he wasn't crazy about it either. Another copy went to Georges Borchardt in New York, and he wrote back within a week to say that, while he "found the book impeccably written," he expected to have "trouble placing it in New York." The writer resisted the urge to reply that "impeccably written" books probably always have trouble in the marketplace, but what the agent really meant was that small-town Ontario and a story with a hockey player in it might not be a good fit for the American market. At least the agent hadn't suggested that he change Buddy Wheeler into a baseball player growing up in Wyoming or Minnesota.

In his own country, Seal Books had published *Sunset Manor* and so had first refusal rights for this book, which they exercised by turning it down. No one likes to be rejected, so when Janet Turnbull conveyed these tidings, he was surprised by her elation with the news. She then told him that she had been hoping all along that Seal would reject the book because she felt that it deserved a bigger publisher, and she had already sent a copy to a highly respected house with a literary reputation, spearheaded by a colourful, opinionated editor who was taking the manuscript with her while she attended a conference in Florida. That was in early November, and weeks passed without a word. He felt he had been left "twisting in the wind," the inevitable fate of middle-aged novelists who haven't scaled the best-seller lists or, for that matter, published a book recently. The watchword of his day now seemed to be "Shut up and wait." Which of course is what he did until a few days before Christmas, when he decided that after six weeks an innocent inquiry could not possibly be construed as unduly bothersome. Somewhat embarrassed, Janet informed him that the CEO had indeed carried his manuscript to Florida and back again but hadn't yet got around to reading it. But more dismaying news awaited him. Upon her return from Disneyland she had passed the manuscript to a junior editor who had written a negative report. Yet his immensely appealing and optimistic agent told him not to worry. She was confident that his book would find a home, and she had already sent the manuscript to Phyllis Bruce at HarperCollins.

Tuesday, January 11, 1994—Miserably depressed all day and then the good news. Phyllis Bruce at HarperCollins loves the book and wants to make an offer.

The only drawback to this delightful reprieve from melancholia was the news that the book could not be fitted into HarperCollins's publishing schedule until the spring of 1995. A year away, but that was all right. He had now reached a point, common enough in most writers' lives, when, after one has published nothing for three or four years, people pass along greetings, always ending with the conversational coda "Are you still writing?" As if not publishing a book every year or two demonstrates a deplorable indolence. Now at least he could say, "Yes, I am still writing and will have a new book coming out next year."

He would be forever grateful to Phyllis Bruce for her faith in that book, now called *The Age of Longing*. At fifty-seven he had sometimes thought that with all the delay and rejection he might be finished as a novelist. He hadn't published anything in nearly five years and his backlist was out of print, so her faith in that book and in him revived his writing life by providing the confidence he needed to continue. And ahead lay pleasant surprises for both of them. During that year awaiting publication he was already thinking of another novel. For whatever reasons, he had not yet finished with either the 1930s or his interest in the lives of unmarried female schoolteachers. Why was that? he often asked himself. Was it because even as a small boy he had wondered about such women who lived without men or families, women from his childhood school days, Miss Jones, Miss McGrath, Miss McMullen, Miss Wagg? Somewhere in his imagination was another schoolteacher, a woman in her thirties living in a village in a house that looked very like his grandparents' house in Woodville, Ontario, where he used to spend the last weeks of the summer holidays. He knew that one day he would tell her story.

Meantime *The Age of Longing* was published in late March of 1995 in a handsome edition that for him captured perfectly the book's wistful melancholy. It received some good reviews and he gave the readings and the media interviews that are part of a writer's life.

All writers are greedy for acclaim, but most don't get any. None. Ever. A thought to spend some time with for anyone contemplating a life with words. He was pleased enough then when

Andrew, Dad and Christopher at Chris's wedding in 1995.

his eighth novel proved a modest success with both the critics and the reading public. Would he have liked his book to have attracted more attention? Of course. Who wouldn't? But by now he knew well enough that, unless written by best-selling authors or literary superstars, most novels have remarkably brief lives, often disappearing a few months after publication, their writers returning to the quotidian world of their own making. In his case to boarding school routines, where one afternoon in early October in the school's hallway he was looking at athletic notices for the intramural soccer schedule when someone tapped his shoulder. There was a phone call for him in the English Department office from his editor Phyllis Bruce. When he called back, she could scarcely contain her excitement in telling him that *The Age of Longing* had been shortlisted for the Giller Prize.

The Giller Prize was then in its second year, but already it had attracted considerable media interest, not only because at $25,000 it was the country's richest literary prize, but also because its founder, Jack Rabinovitch, wanted the Giller to be celebrated with a glittering dinner at the Four Seasons Hotel in Toronto. It was a brilliant idea, and the Giller Gala, as it was soon called, became the hottest ticket in town, a glamorous event in the service of literature. He was just happy to be invited.

A few days later he had more good news from Phyllis Bruce: his book had also been shortlisted for the Governor General's Award. He and Barbara Gowdy were the only two authors that year who had been nominated for both awards. He can remember saying to his wife, "My cup runneth over." To which she replied, "It's about time, don't you think?"

As it turned out, neither he nor Gowdy would win either award that year. The Giller went to Rohinton Mistry for *A Fine Balance,* and the Governor General's Award for fiction to Greg Hollingshead for *The Roaring Girl.* As for the party at the Four Seasons? It was an evening of good-natured conversation and laughter, and at one point he and a fellow finalist, Tiff Findley, found themselves literally "under the table" on hands and knees; not from too much wine, but in search of an earring dropped by his wife, which Tiff found, arising finally with a triumphant cry. "Aha. I found the little devil!"

Finding Clara

His ninth novel, *Clara Callan*, would take nearly five years to finish, but it was worth all that time and effort. In 2001 it was well received both critically and commercially at home and abroad. It won the Giller Prize, the Governor General's Award and the Trillium Book Award. Two years later, on the tenth anniversary of the Giller, the decade's prize winners were invited to submit a brief essay on some aspect of their book: its origins or inspiration, its composition. These reflections were published by the Giller Prize Foundation in a book presented as a gift to guests at that year's anniversary dinner. Under one cover was a compendium of observations on the craft of writing; on the trials and tribulations, the heartburn and hurrahs of the roller-coaster ride from blank page to prize-winning book. His contribution was entitled "Finding Clara."

Author and Governor General Adrienne Clarkson
at awards ceremony, 2001.

Author and Governor General Michaëlle Jean
at the Order of Canada investiture, 2007.

FINDING CLARA

At a recent book signing, I was approached by a young man who gave me a hopeful smile and said, "Now that you've written several novels, it must get easier." I was not exactly aghast, but perilously close, wondering if a suitably witty and sarcastic aperçu might be in order. Something like "Hell yes, once you get the hang of it, there's nothing to it." But being a good Canadian, mindful of my manners even when asked a dumb question, I merely looked tormented, shrugged and muttered, "Not necessarily."

Later, however, thinking about it, I had to admit that the young man's question was more artless than gormless. Many people might ask the same question, and why not? Most things we do in life become easier with practice; in everything from sex to saxophone playing we learn from our mistakes, and we tend not to waste time and energy on things we know we cannot do. So why wouldn't the same principle apply to writing novels? In many cases it would seem to; in certain genres, like detective fiction, for example, novelists like Agatha Christie and Georges Simenon with their off-the-rack characters and familiar settings must have found writing easier as the years passed.

But what of those who inhabit another fictional landscape and labour in other vineyards? For the sake of convenience, let's call them writers of literary fiction. For such folk, it's questionable whether the task gets easier. Our patron saint is Sisyphus, with his hill, his rock and his bursitis. The harsh truth is that the fourteenth book (if you have the *cojones* to imagine such a preposterous undertaking) will very likely be just as difficult as the third or fourth. If not more so. Headaches will abound and the long face will be seen in the land.

Of all my novels, for example, my ninth, *Clara Callan*, was undoubtedly the most difficult to write. It also took the longest time, nearly five years, and although it was written around a teaching job, so were others that took fewer years off my life. As proof I offer a few random notes from journals, kept under lock and key lest they fall into the wrong hands and my lazy and infrequent observations be revealed for what they are, a perfunctory record of banality ("Today was sunny and cool. Humidity gone, winds light. N.W."). Still they didn't call them commonplace books for nothing, and a journal of this and that, however poorly maintained, can be useful in settling family disputes about where a summer holiday was spent in 1982. And for a writer who has lost his way in the middle of a book, a journal can also remind him of how sorely pressed he was while writing other novels. Our memories tend to severely edit both pain and joy; somehow they have to be set down in words to remind us of what they really felt like.

I am seldom cheerful about work in progress; I'm something of an Eeyore who, when asked, "How's the book going?" is apt to mumble, "It's going," often adding, helpfully, "sort of." Yet in rereading journal entries from 1996 to 2000, I am still astonished not only at how difficult it was for me to capture the essence of what I was after, but also at how frequently I was discouraged by the book's lack of progress, its damnable waywardness. All that, of course, was ahead of me as I plunged in on the second Monday of January 1996.

Monday, January 8, 1996
Began a novel today. A working title. 1943. Story about a 12-year-old girl who runs away from a boarding school with her eccentric grandmother to NYC. Middle of the War.

Sunday, January 28
This isn't working. I'm thinking of another approach. A diary form. The girl's voice with a detached narrator. Half sister?

Tuesday, January 30
Lucy Callan—that's the girl's name.

Tuesday, February 6
The original idea is wrong somehow, and I don't feel comfortable with it. A different book emerging. Two sisters and the birth of radio. The Talking Box Lady or Radioland. Something like that.

Tuesday, April 9
See the book now as a monologue in which a PhD candidate interviews Nora Callan on her early days in radio for his thesis on popular culture: the effects of radio on commercial civilization, etc. Add scripts, letters, etc.

I was obviously floundering, and things didn't improve as summer approached. I had been looking forward to ten weeks in which I could write most of the day, instead of the two-hour morning shift. But it was not to be; at about the time I was settling in, suddenly there was giant bulldozer and dump truck action in the neighbourhood. The foundation of our house was shuddering. Something to do with sewer pipes under our street. By the end of July, I had thrown in the pen, and, although I didn't admit as much, I probably welcomed the excuse.

I couldn't seem to find my way into the story. I was spending too much time with this Ph.D. character talking to Nora about the early days of radio. I had also decided that these interviews were taking place in the summer of 1969, which was the summer the Manson gang murdered Sharon Tate and others in Los Angeles. All that crazy stuff was working its way into the story. Perhaps I was looking for some kind of contrast between Nora's 1930s and the anarchic 1960s. In any case, the book was definitely getting weirder by the day. In October I was still flailing away, and the following entry eloquently describes my frustration.

Friday, October 4
I feel I'm really back to square one. On the other hand, I might just have something worth pursuing. I just have to relax and write the fucking thing.

Grave doubts, however, continued to linger well into 1997.

Sunday, April 20
Reached p. 98.
This is a very slow process, and I'm not sure that it is working . . .

All that spring and summer I was reading microfilm of the L.A. papers with their coverage of the Manson murders and the subsequent investigation. There before me was the whole nutty

L.A. scene in 1969, and I was like some kind of news junkie, overdosing on mayhem and spectacular chaos: Charlie and his goofy women drugged out of their skulls, the orgies at the farm, the city of angels engulfed in smog and death. The end of the world. I think the California sun was getting to me. This, I decided, was not my story. Hunter S. Thompson's maybe, but not mine. I had to trash it all, and that hurt because I had put a lot of work into it, and some of it was OK. Maybe even better than OK. Or so I thought at the time.

There were, however, positive signs. By the end of the year, I had nearly three hundred pages, and I had shifted the focus away from Nora to Clara, who was a much more interesting person to write about with her anxieties and doubts, her complicated nature. I had given Nora a glamorous boyfriend, a Jewish gangster named Max somebody-or-other who had once worked for Big Bill Dwyer, a Prohibition bootlegger who used to own the old New York Americans hockey team. More time was lost going down that road before Max got the cut. Meanwhile I was wondering if I was spending my earthly hours wisely.

Wednesday, November 26
"Nothing should be more highly prized than the value of each day." Goethe

Exactly, Johann. So what the hell am I doing down here at five in the morning?

Yet on New Year's Eve, perhaps in a celebratory humour, I had given my eponymous heroine a new name and was clinging to a thread of hope.

Wednesday, December 31
The name Lucy is too jaunty for her temperament. Call her
Clara. A big job ahead and I would be lying if I said I wasn't
discouraged. Still I can see possibilities in this book. As long
as there are possibilities . . .

The American writer Bernard Malamud once described writing a novel as a long voyage in a small room. The metaphor of a
journey is certainly apt, but the voyager is often without a reliable map, or indeed any map at all; moreover, it is a journey that
must be measured at least in months and more likely in years.
Unlike the lyric poet, or the short-story writer, the novelist has
no chance whatsoever of experiencing that epiphanic glow that
might arise from completing something in a matter of hours or
days. Like a long-distance runner, he has to pace himself, tem-
pering his emotional reaction to a day's work, becoming neither
unduly elated over what he perceives to be terrific stuff nor un-
reasonably depressed over what looks like a wrong turning. All
that, of course, is easier said than done, as this entry from the
spring of 1999 will attest.

Saturday, May 8
Attacked by a total loss of confidence in this thing. Walked
away from the book at 9:30 and went downtown for a haircut.

Yet by then the book had assumed a life of its own; I was
inside the world of my characters, and I was often happy there.
Over the next year and a half, my inclination to believe that
things would not work out—that I could not solve certain

problems—was offset by the growing sense that I was slowly gaining control over my material.

I suspect that most serious writers live in a more or less constant state of discontent while labouring on their manuscripts. Hubris is for amateurs. Not long ago at a party, I was cornered by a fellow who was perhaps the cousin of the young man at the book signing; at least he seemed to have the same kind of naïveté in his DNA. This took place in the host's kitchen, where thankfully I found myself adjacent to a jeroboam of vodka. The fellow began to recount in marvelous detail the characters and events in the novel he was working on, offering as well his confident expectation of the book's appearance one day on major prize lists, etc., etc. I listened, only mildly horrified, waiting for the gods to strike him dead or, perhaps in a mood of Ovidian playfulness, transform him into a screenwriter in Hollywood, where, I'm told, the denizens traffic openly in delusional tales and outrageous optimism.

In December 2000 I finished the book. My editor, Phyllis Bruce, liked it and made some sensible suggestions for its improvement. *Clara Callan* was published the following September.

Richard and Phyllis on the *Queen Mary 2* in 2005.

Phyllis in South of France, 2008.

What Happens When
We Read Stories

Over the next few years, he would publish three more novels, *Adultery*, *October* and *Mr. Shakespeare's Bastard*. In 2007, he was inducted as a member into the Order of Canada for his contribution to Canadian literature.

He had retired from teaching in 2001, the year *Clara Callan* was published. By then his wife was head of the Reference Department at Brock University and they felt more financially secure. But he had also begun to suspect that his entire approach to teaching English was coming under siege from a culture utterly enthralled by technology. At the school there were frequent workshops and seminars on the role of the computer in the classrooms. He was admittedly not a fan of computer-driven curricula, though he recognized that in time they would be inevitable. Still he was amused by the cheerleading of so many of his colleagues and the administration, who saw only great advances in the classrooms of the future. As for him, he saw only an increase in distractions and reduced attention spans with students playing games and sending messages to one another. Perhaps it was time to go.

The year before he had been delighted to be asked by Brock University to accept an honorary doctorate of letters, the first of three such academic honours he would receive. In his address to the graduating students at the Fall Convocation in that first year of the new century, he spoke of his concerns about a world that was becoming more and more dependent on technology, not only in the classroom but also in virtually every aspect of ordinary life. In an increasingly visual age, he wondered if we were not about to lose something vital; namely our capacity to utilize and appreciate the narrative imagination. His remarks were mostly directed toward film and television, but the Age of the Internet was already well under way, and his reservations about the impact of it all on narrative were underlined in his address to the students and faculty.

WHAT HAPPENS WHEN WE READ STORIES

For a few minutes, I'd like to talk to you on a subject that is close to my heart, namely reading. And I am thinking especially of a particular type of reading—the reading of stories and the value of the narrative imagination.

Everyone is familiar with the benefits of reading to acquire information: we read in order to write essays and pass examinations; we read to unravel the mysterious instructions for assembling, say, a new lawn mower or stereo system. The day-to-day practical uses of reading then are obvious to everyone. What I am more interested in, however, is reading for something else: for diversion, for pleasure, for understanding. And it seems to me that in a culture that is becoming increasingly dependent on the visual, this kind of reading is under siege. There are unmistakable signs, particularly in the young, that we are losing a certain habit of mind and along with that, perhaps, something else.

In an interview in the *New Yorker* magazine, American novelist Philip Roth spoke of the decline of what we might call literary reading. He said,

> *The evidence is everywhere that the literary era has come to an end. The evidence is the culture, the evidence is the society, the evidence is the screen, the progression from the movie screen to the television screen to the computer . . . Literature takes a habit of mind that has disappeared. It*

requires silence, some form of isolation and sustained con-
centration in the presence of an enigmatic thing.

Perhaps Roth was being a little too gloomy about the future
of reading and literature, but certainly he had underlined the
tendency of our electronic culture to bypass the printed word.

Now I am going to take it as a given that we all need stories.
Even the most obdurate engineer or math student is kidding
himself or herself with the declaration that "I have no time for
that make-believe stuff." Well, you can take it for granted that
our young engineer or mathematician goes to the movies now
and then, or watches television comedies or dramas just like the
rest of us. Like everyone else, they too are interested in stories;
it's just that they receive and process narrative visually. They
watch stories, rather than read them. There seems to be, within
all of us, an inescapable need for narrative. In whatever form we
receive them, stories are as necessary to our emotional health
as companionship and love. Why this is so is a mystery, but it
is undeniably so and it is the rare person who goes through life
without some curiosity about how people, even imaginary people, deal with their problems or enjoy their triumphs.

As Roth alludes to, however, our tendency more and more
is to watch stories rather than read them. The reason is simple.
Watching is easier than reading, which requires, to use Roth's
expression, "a habit of mind," a conscious effort to arrange our
days so that there is time to take what is admittedly a more difficult path through the story. A hundred years ago, a man or a
woman at the end of their day might sit down to read; in our
time they are more likely to turn on the TV. As a species, for
better or worse (and let's face it, it's been mostly better), we

worship daily at the altar of convenience. There isn't one of us here who hasn't said at the end of a particularly trying day, "Oh, I just feel like vegging out in front of the box tonight." So, we take a shortcut into narrative; we don't have to deal so much with the words; we can just sit back and watch. Now there is nothing especially baleful about this, yet I can't help wondering if constant and passive submission to the visual doesn't weaken and atrophy our imaginations, make us less open somehow to authentic experience. So *what happens when we read stories that doesn't happen when we watch them?*

Let me tell you a story about two very different young women. One lives in a high-rise apartment in Toronto at the beginning of the twenty-first century; the other lived in a fishing village in the west of Ireland in the eighth century. One will read a story and the other will write one. Let us imagine for a moment a young woman who has graduated from university, say three years ago. Let us make her a biology major who now works for a large pharmaceutical company in Toronto. The young woman's academic strengths have obviously been in the maths and sciences; she has never really had much interest in reading, especially stories or novels. She vaguely recalls English classes in high school when she was made to read these things and then, or so it seemed to her, everyone just talked about them, though to what purpose she never really discovered. There was nothing about that side of her education that she found demonstrably useful. She does, however, like some television shows and she enjoys going to the movies, though she wishes so many of them nowadays weren't so childishly violent, or so ingratiatingly sentimental.

One night she works late, and on the way home, in the swaying, nearly empty subway car, she sees on the seat next to her a book of stories. She picks it up and takes it home to her apartment and it sits forgotten on her dresser for two weeks. Then one night when television doesn't seem to offer anything of much interest, and her friends are occupied, she picks up this book and opens it to a story called "The Lady with the Pet Dog." The young woman likes the title because she likes dogs, but as she begins to read, she soon realizes that the story is not about dogs at all; it is, in fact, a love story set in southern Russia over a hundred years ago. A middle-aged womanizer named Gurov sees a young woman named Anna walking her little dog. Both are on vacation at a seaside town called Yalta in the Crimea. Gurov plans to use his charms and considerable experience to seduce Anna; she will become another of his conquests. All this was written many years ago by a Russian doctor named Anton Chekhov.

It is late and the noise of the city settles and fades into the night. Our young biology graduate sits under the reading lamp in her apartment. The light spills across the pages of the book in her hands. At first it is hard going; all those long Russian names, the leisurely pace of the story, all those words. Yet as she reads, she cannot deny that there is something compelling in the voice of the writer, the dead Russian writer whose words are entering the mind of this young woman in a Canadian city. She has never been to Yalta in the heat of summer or to Moscow in the depth of winter, but in her mind she can now see these landscapes against which the lovers are playing out their drama. So there is just the young woman and the dead Russian writer's words and the late-night silence in her apartment. What is happening as she reads is that she is being directly addressed by another human being. In her mind's eye she can see Gurov and Anna walking together through the summer evening, talking of the "strange light on the sea." There is no swelling music to signal an impending change of mood, no celebrity face to stare at; just words transforming into images in her mind. She finds that she has time to reflect on the fates of these two people who are both on the perilous edge of deception and adultery. How will it all turn out? She senses that, unlike most stories that she watches, it will not end happily. But that doesn't seem to matter, and, when she comes to the end of the story, she is a little saddened, but in another way moved. Yes, that is the way life sometimes is, she thinks, and it must be acknowledged. She feels that having been in the presence of these two imaginary people for an hour or so, she has encountered an authentic experience free of manipulation and contrivance. The writer has invited her into the world he has imagined, and she has shared the experience of participating in it.

Art critic Robert Hughes has reflected on the differences between reading and watching, and he writes,

> *Reading is a collaborative act in which your imagination goes halfway to meet the author's; you visualize the book as you read it; you participate in making up the characters and rounding them out. . . . The effort of bringing something vivid out of the neutral array of black print is quite different and in my experience, far better for the imagination than passive submission to the bright icons of television which come complete and overwhelming, and tend to burn out the tender wiring of a child's imagination because they allow no re-working.*

Hughes is directly addressing the problems that affect children when reading is replaced by watching. But the warning, I think, stands for all of us. We all know how difficult it is to erase the vast and peculiar radiance of the film image when we read a book *after* we have seen a movie version of it. I remember watching the film *Out of Africa* before I read the book. I thought it was a wonderful movie and I enjoyed it very much; yet, when I came to read Isak Dinesen's intelligent and luminous account of her life in Africa in the early years of the twentieth century, I kept running into Robert Redford and Meryl Streep. So powerful and seductive are these glamorous images that they simply overwhelm our imaginations.

Am I suggesting that we stop going to movies and stop watching television drama? Of course not. The various wonders of our age must be duly regarded and celebrated. What I am suggesting, however, is that we are in danger of losing something precious and vital to the human spirit, namely our capacity to receive stories that are unadulterated, stories that have not been compromised by vanity or commerce.

Let me end with a story about another young woman, the one who lived in a fishing village in the west of Ireland in the eighth century. We know nothing about this young woman. We know only what she tells us in her story, which comes to us across hundreds of years in the form of a poem in which she addresses the young man whom she loves, a young man who has made promises he hasn't kept, a young man who probably seduced her and has now left her forsaken and alone. I like to imagine this young woman fashioning the words of her story as she mends her father's fishing nets, or watches the sheep on the hillside, or walks to Mass on Sunday morning in the rain. Who taught her to write? I wonder. And how did she get it down on paper? What kind of paper? A page torn from her missal? How did she conceal these words from her mother and father? We shall never know. But write she did, one poem, truthful and everlasting, her words crossing many centuries to reach us, a voice speaking to us. The poem is called "Donal Og." The author is anonymous. The translation is by Lady Gregory.

It is late last night the dog was speaking of you;
the snipe was speaking of you in her deep marsh.
It is you are the lonely bird through the woods;
and that you may be without a mate until you find me.

You promised me, and you said a lie to me,
that you would be before me where the sheep are flocked;
I gave a whistle and three hundred cries to you,
and I found nothing there but a bleating lamb.

You promised me a thing that was hard for you,
a ship of gold under a silver mast;
twelve towns with a market in all of them,
and a fine white court by the side of the sea.

You promised me a thing that is not possible,
that you would give me gloves of the skin of a fish;
that you would give me shoes of the skin of a bird;
and a suit of the dearest silk in Ireland.

When I go by myself to the Well of Loneliness,
I sit down and I go through my troubles;
when I see the world and do not see my boy,
he that has an amber shade in his hair.

It was on that Sunday I gave my love to you;
the Sunday that is last before Easter Sunday.
And myself on my knees reading the Passion;
and my two eyes giving love to you for ever.

My mother said to me not to be talking with you today,
or tomorrow, or on the Sunday;
it was a bad time she took for telling me that;
it was shutting the door after the house was robbed.

My heart is as black as the blackness of the sloe,
or as the black coat that is on the smith's forge;
or as the sole of a shoe left in white halls;
it was you that put that darkness over my life.

You have taken the east from me; you have taken the west
*   from me;*
you have taken what is before me and what is behind me;
you have taken the moon, you have taken the sun from me;
and my fear is great that you have taken God from me!

At first it would be easy to be disheartened by such a plaintive cry. Yet like all good stories, it is there to remind us of the human adventure that we call life, and of the ever-present and uneasy alliance between disappointment and hope. It is experience conveyed truthfully in language we can all understand. *What happens when we read stories that doesn't happen when we watch them?* It's simple really. We encounter another human being speaking to us; our imaginations are revitalized by words as we fashion them into ideas and images, not images manufactured by others and forever calcified, but our own and singular images, the images of our own making. We are also allowed to pause and reflect on what has happened. To muse. To ponder. To accept the quiet of thought. The symbiotic relationship between the writer and the reader is vital and active, unhampered by the glamour of the screen, and free from the manipulation and compromise that inevitably accompany visual storytelling.

We are the only species on earth with a language complex enough to name our world, to convey ideas, to express our innermost feelings. Without words we are reduced in our capacity to endure vicissitudes or express our wonder at being alive.